MAILLOL

BERTRAND LORQUIN

ARISTIDE
MAILLOL

IN ASSOCIATION WITH
THAMES AND HUDSON

To John Rewald

The author wishes to express his gratitude
to Araxie Toutghalian for her assistance.

Conception   Jean-Luc Daval
Layout   Estelle Daval
Translation   Michael Taylor

First published in Great Britain in 1995 by
Thames and Hudson Ltd, London

First published in the United States of America in 1995 by
Thames and Hudson Inc., 500 Fifth Avenue, New York, New York 10110

British Library Cataloguing-in-Publication Data

A catalogue record for this book is available from the British Library

ISBN 0-500-97417-9

Library of Congress Catalog Card Number: 94-61693

Printed and bound in Switzerland

CONTENTS

Introduction

by Dina Vierny

The present volume is the first major monograph on Aristide Maillol. There is of course John Rewald's excellent book, published in Paris in 1939; and there is Judith Cladel's biography, a book of undeniable sincerity. It was my privilege to have been acquainted with both historians, and I know for a fact that Maillol was pleased with both works. But these books have long been out of print, and there has been an increasingly urgent need for a fresh, up-to-date look at Maillol and a new analysis of his œuvre.

Maillol was inspired by great ideas. There was nothing ordinary about him. He was an inventor. Where other artists have been content to try their hand at ceramics, he devised a new kind of glazed terracotta. He disliked drawing on commercially available paper, so he developed his own paper with a watermark of his own design. Montval paper caught on and still exists.

In sculpture, he simplified form, did away with movement, opened up that art to silence. He rediscovered simplicity and was, with the Cubists, one of the pioneers of abstraction and modernism in sculpture.

La Méditerranée, 1923-1927 — Marble — H. 110.5 cm — Paris, Musée d'Orsay

Like Renoir, he disliked theories. It is unfortunate that he left no writings on art: he had a talent for expressing his ideas with brevity, clarity, and eloquence.

I am always amazed by the aptness of Octave Mirbeau's description of him in 1905, and by the fact that Mirbeau's words still applied when Maillol was an old man.

He was labelled a "revolutionary," but never took the word seriously, which is a great pity. I recall seeing him laugh at his biographer Judith Clavel when, at Marly in the summer of 1938, Rodin's white-haired former companion called him this. He often poked fun at people, as well as at himself – and at the passing years, which seemed to have no hold on him. He was not someone who took himself overly seriously.

André Gide, Maurice Denis, Rodin, Meier-Graefe, Kenneth Clarke, and John Rewald are unfortunately no longer with us to speak about his art. Too often Maillol's contribution to modernity is forgotten. All too often he is remembered merely as a rhapsodist of womanhood.

Having towered above his century, Maillol died in 1944. It is not easy for people born after the war to understand how fundamental a difference there was between traditional art and the new currents in pre-war art.

Nor was it simple for Maillol, who fought against academicism all his life, to get himself accepted in a world where academic art was still a force to be reckoned with. In spite of his worldwide renown, he was never an official sculptor in France.

In 1994, fifty years after his death, major exhibitions of his œuvre are being held around the world. The Maillol Museum in Paris is at last opening its doors.

In the mountain country where he loved to live and work, amid one of the most beautiful landscapes in the world – as he himself was fond of pointing out – a scenery comparable to Sicily and Greece; in the clearing where he worked *en plein air* with his model and where he now rests beneath his favorite sculpture, *La Méditerranée*, stands a modest iconographic museum, which seems to emerge from his native soil in order to tell the story of his œuvre and the part it plays in twentieth-century art.

Easter 1994

CHAPTER I

Maillol the painter
The origins of his œuvre

Born under the Second Empire, Maillol came of age at a turning point between two eras. He started out as a Nabi painter in the 1890s, but made his mark as a sculptor in our own century. His œuvre is a radical departure from neoclassical and academic art, and, concurrently with Cubism but before abstraction, it opened up a new perspective in modern art. Moreover, Maillol revolutionized the art of sculpture by creating a type of beauty which, in his tireless quest for harmony, he explored in all its forms.

Maillol was born in 1861 into a family of farmers established in Banyuls, a small olive and wine growing village in the south of France, with its back to the Pyrenees and its feet washed, so to speak, by the Mediterranean. A country at once harsh and generous, it shaped his personality. All his life, he kept returning to live and work in his birthplace. His aunts owned a house in the center of the village, surrounded by a garden in which a spreading fig tree casts its shade. It was here

The Crowned Child, 1890
Oil on canvas
47 x 40 cm

that he spent his first years as a child. His father, a draper, had frequent commercial dealings with Algeria where his sisters ran a thriving retail shop. Often abroad, he took little part in the education of his five children. Left to cope by herself, his wife preferred to entrust young Aristide's schooling to her in-laws.

Maillol was thus raised by his grandfather and, chiefly, his aunt Lucie. He attended the village school and appears to have been a solitary child. He spent most of his time out-of-doors, roaming in vineyards, catching butterflies and other insects, and collecting sea shells on the beach. His love for objects cast up by the sea was to stay with him and, later, he would pick up pieces of rusty iron on the sand and use them to make armatures for his sculptures. He once told his childhood friend, Dr. Bassères, that the Catalonian soil was the first, inexhaustible source of his inspiration: "My village, which I love more than anything I have ever seen, has every resource to offer a painter – it's as if a golden dust had been scattered over the entire area."[1]

His aunt Lucie enrolled him in a boarding school in nearby Perpignan, the Collège Saint-Louis. The curriculum included drawing

Self-Portrait, 1888
Oil on canvas
32 x 24 cm

lessons, though they were primarily designed to develop technical skills that could be put to use in industry. Maillol's first painting dates from this period, a small view of the port at Banyuls. The desire to pursue an artistic career came to him fairly early, and he was soon taking private lessons from his drawing teacher and copying paintings in Perpignan's Hyacinthe Rigaud Museum.

At twenty, Maillol decided to devote himself entirely to art and, against his family's wishes,

left for Paris. He found lodgings near one of his former teachers, and applied for admission to the École des Beaux-Arts. He was turned down, as Rodin had been earlier. He studied painting and sculpture at the Arts Décoratifs and attended the Beaux-Arts as an auditor. He met Achille Laugé in Cabanel's atelier, as well as Antoine Bourdelle. Southerners all three, they soon became fast friends. Maillol also attended the classes of Gérome, the leading heir to the Ingres tradition. Though disappointed by the mediocre quality of academic teaching, he nevertheless managed to acquire a solid technical background. Many years later, he was to say that it was "Gauguin and Maurice Denis who opened my eyes after I left the École... The lot of someone who arrives in Paris hoping to follow an artistic career is pretty grim... The poor wretch tumbles into the Ecole as though it was a well. He doesn't find the truth there, because in fact it's outside!"[2]

While still a student, he exhibited two paintings at the Salon des Artistes Français: a landscape painted in 1888 and the 1890 portrait of Jeanne Faraill. Two years earlier he had done a self-portrait in the manner of Courbet. The only self-portrait of Maillol's that we know of, it recalls the words of Octave Mirbeau's description of the young artist: "With his pointed face, his bright darting eyes, his sharp nose that always seems to be sniffing something, his

Portrait of Aunt Lucie
Oil on canvas
171 x 128 cm

smooth, loose-limbed, careful way of walking, he resembles a young wolf. Coming straight from the masses, he has never disowned his noble peasant birth. On the contrary, he flaunts it. (…) His soul is as transparent as that of someone who has never been troubled by evil desires. His speech is picturesque and graceful and his words are simple, strong, true, colorful, and memorable."[3]

Maillol's palette during these years was dark, and his brush strokes were characterized by a fondness for impasto, which he was very soon to grow out of. He was beginning to move away from the brown earth tones favored by Courbet. "I stopped imitating him," he declared in later years, "because I knew intuitively that I would never have his power." Feeling very isolated, he turned toward the work of other artists he admired, such as Puvis de Chavannes, whose *Poor Fisherman* — a painting which left a mark on an entire generation — he copied. It was in the same spirit that, during a brief return to Banyuls, he painted his first large-scale canvas, the *Portrait of Aunt Lucie,* with its flat, even treatment, which Gauguin found rather dry. The 1880s were particularly difficult years for Maillol from the financial standpoint. He got by with the help of a grant from the Council of his native Department of the Pyrénées-Orientales and a small allowance from his aunt.

At the Beaux-Arts, Maillol met the painter Daniel de Monfreid who persuaded him in 1889 to join him at the Café Volpini, an establishment within the grounds of the Universal Exposition, where he was exhibiting his work jointly with Gauguin and other friends (Schuffenecker, Anquetin, Emile Bernard, Laval, Fauché, and Louis Roy). Proclaiming themselves the "Impressionist and Synthetist Group," these artists had boycotted the official exhibition and were promoting their own aesthetic creed. Closer in spirit to Symbolism than to Realism, it was based on Gauguin's pictorial principles of eliminating perspective and laying down unmixed pigments in flat colored areas in order to build a synthesis. The critic Gustave Geffroy commented thus on this unofficial group show: "What appears to unite these artists in a common quest is chiefly their preoccupation with a linear synthesis and their violent splashes of color. Using the formula of drawing the most plastic and dynamic arabesques, the Japanese made figures that look as if they sprang spontaneously from a single line."[4] This style was later to be labeled *Cloisonnisme.*

This pictorial renaissance corresponded to what Maillol, disenchanted with the academic teaching at the Beaux-Arts, was looking for. It enabled him to appropriate the modernity and liberating abstraction of *Japonisme* (which had also helped Gauguin to break new ground in painting). Though it owed nothing to the Nabi painters, this discovery occurred around the same time as their discovery of the Japanese printmakers. Gauguin's painting was a revelation to Maillol, and the older artist's influence on the student still searching for his own expression proved to be decisive.

Mademoiselle Faraill Wearing a Hat, 1890
Oil on canvas
46.5 x 55.5 cm

Light tones soon dominated Maillol's palette. Color defined the underlying structure of his compositions and molded their forms, as well as their light and the perception of time they expressed. Each color seemed to throb with a desire to encompass the picture as a whole. Maillol's painting was increasingly shaped by his striving to achieve a pictorial synthesis – in other words to come up with a form, a technique, a plastic equivalent for (rather than a sign illustrating) a feeling or human thought. He rejected literary Symbolism and the art of allegory. Several of his 1890 paintings are compositions of young women rendered in

Seated Woman with Parasol, 1895
Oil on canvas
148 x 18 cm

profile against a floral decor. "His art is essentially an art of synthesis. Though not drawn to it by any theory, or by anything other than his own instinct, he took part in the neoclassical movement whose recent origin lay in Cézanne and Gauguin and their circles. (...) It was the expression of the synthetist rebelling against the eclectic realism of academies which awakened the true nature of Cabanel's student, Maillol."[5]

In the spirit of the great tradition of portrait painting from Piero Della Francesca and Pisanello to the silhouettes of the eighteenth century, Maillol rendered his portraits in profile, as

Woman with Parasol, ca. 1900 – Oil on canvas – 190 x 149 cm – Paris, Musée d'Orsay

The Two Young Girls, 1890 – Oil on canvas – 59 x 105 cm

Woman's Profile, 1896
Pastel and charcoal
34 x 46 cm

Young Girl Wearing Black Hat, ca. 1890
Oil on canvas
55.5 x 46 cm

if they were expressions of "inner modelling."
Outlined against a luminous, abstract, uniform
background, *The Crowned Child* belongs to this
dream world.

Maillol's treatment of the background
in juxtaposed brushstrokes which establish a
flat plane is characteristic of modern portrait
painting. The full-length *Woman with Parasol*
is profiled against horizontal bands defining
grass, sand, sea, and sky. The totally simplified landscape accentuates the presence
of this *plein air* figure standing out against
a background that suggests space without
depth.

The quest for a pictorial synthesis, the rendering by means of flat areas, and the decorative resolve also characterize the work of the Nabis, a group of painters who had trained at the Académie Julian in Paris. (They received their name, which means "prophet" in Hebrew, from the poet Cazalis.) Their ranks included Bonnard, Vuillard, Maurice Denis, Ranson, Vallotton, Verkade, and Rippl-Rónai, who introduced Maillol into their circle. Gauguin's ideas made a great impact on these young artists, via Sérusier's *The Talisman* (1888), which the younger artist had painted under Gauguin's supervision. The Nabis were Neoplatonists: they regarded a work of art as the expression of an idea made perceptible by its form. Form mediated between the visible and the invisible, reality and dream. Painting was the art of revealing the image that lies on the surface of every tangible object. The artist's task was to recreate the feeling of a whole world on a flat plane, to give a palpable form to his subjectivity and inner universe. The 1896 *Woman's Profile* represents a girl absorbed in a daydream. In contrast to the Symbolists, Maillol used neither signs nor emblems. He replaced allegories with arabesques, charging them with a symbolic function so that, as stylistic forms, they were able to transform reality and metamorphose women into ideas. In *Seated Woman with Parasol* he combined meticulous arabesques with colored impressions translating the interplay of light and shadow. While retaining all the qualities of a flat decorative surface, this canvas nevertheless suggests a great depth of field. It treats nature as a texture, a wallpaper splashed with sunlight, its subtle contrasts of shade and illumination transforming the garden in which the young woman is seated into a decorative texture comparable to Vuillard's *Afternoon in the Luxemburg Gardens.*

The treatment and brushwork of Maillol's painting never stopped evolving. The colors rendered by juxtaposing and dividing strokes somewhat in the manner of Seurat's Divisionism were gradually replaced by more uniform, less scintillating textures. Maillol's range of tones was limited, but he was able to put all its potential to use. The sinuous outline of the face in the *Portrait of Madame Maillol*, the impression of gracefulness produced by the expression and by the overall composition, render not only the sweet gravity of the young woman's features but also a wider sensation encompassing the lines of the face and the branches and foliage in the background. The two sets of lines seem to echo each other, thereby creating a transition from the dimension of immediate sense perceptions to a dimension where the face becomes the landscape of the soul.

Concurrently with his experiments with portraiture, Maillol also painted a number of landscapes. He drew inspiration from the landscapes of his native Midi, with their rich colors and contrasting medley of sunlight and shadows. Though his wife was his only model, he

Portrait of Madame Maillol, 1894
Oil on canvas
42 x 32 cm

began painting nudes and combining the female anatomy with the spectacle of nature. In *La Côte d'Azur*, he includes a nude in a marine landscape. The figure is rendered frontally and the naked body separated from the rest of the composition by an ample drapery.

The Wave may have been intended as a mural or stage decoration. These were years when Maillol, like his Nabi acquaintances, was deeply interested in the theater. He executed décors for Lugné-Poe and Maurice Bouchor's marionette theater. Inspired by one of Gauguin's pictures, *The Wave* represents a female nude from the back, about to be engulfed by a foaming breaker. Transposed to a tapestry and later a sculpture, the painting is also the very first source of *La Méditerranée*.

Again like the Nabis, Maillol succumbed briefly to the temptation to abandon easel painting for mural decoration. Jan Verkade (known to his friends as "le Nabi obéliscal") issued the group's battle cry: "Down with perspective! Walls must remain flat surfaces... What we want is mural decorations, not paintings." Maillol, who had recently discovered the medieval tapestries at the Cluny Museum in

Decorative Tapestry for a Chair, ca. 1900
30 x 75 cm

The Wave, 1898
Oil on canvas
96 x 89 cm
Paris, Musée du Petit Palais

Seated Nude, 1896 – Charcoal – 98.5 x 92.5 cm

The Bather, or The Wave, 1896 – Needlepoint tapestry – 100 x 93 cm

Two Women Sitting in a Garden, ca. 1895
Zincograph
22 x 26.5 cm

Paris, took up that supremely decorative art, tapestry-making. He set up a small workshop in Banyuls with two young seamstresses, the sisters Clotilde and Angèle Narcisse. Tapestry was almost a vanished art at the end of the nineteenth century. The famous Gobelins tapestryworks were using chemical pigments and merely manufacturing copies of cartoons by old masters or imitations of paintings. Maillol considered tapestry the most accomplished form of pictorial art, and revolutionized it. Always highly demanding about the quality of the materials he worked with, he used pure wool and natural dyes. The wool he obtained from Rumania; the dyes he got from plants growing on the hills above Banyuls. A frequent visitor at the Cluny Museum, he examined the tapestries there at length, especially the

Cartoon for Tapestry for Princess Bibesco, ca. 1895
Oil on canvas
46.5 x 56 cm

Lady With Unicorn and *Vie Seigneurial* series (with its two panels, *Le Bain* et *La Femme Jouant au Luth*). He reinterpreted both themes in his own tapestries. Tapestry-making allowed him to invent a world rich in poetic imagery and to give his personal interpretation of the Nabis' program of "turning reality into a dream." His tapestries have a timeless atmosphere which recalls the Neoplatonic ideal of sensuality combined with spirituality, thereby opening up the floodgates of the imagination to the beauty of the physical world. Their compositions are entirely subsumed to the principle of floral decorations, as in the medieval *mille fleurs* tapestries.

Using few tones, Maillol worked essentially at producing a surface effect in the medieval tradition of "respecting the wall." Gauguin nevertheless criticized his first tapestry, declaring, "There must be no perspective" in tapestries.[6] Hung at the Société Nationale Salon, Maillol's second tapestry earned him an invitation to take part in the Salon de la Libre Esthétique in Brussels in 1893. Gauguin wrote in a review of the latter: "Maillol is showing a tapestry which cannot be praised too highly."[7] The tapestry was acquired for 300 francs by the Galerie Druet, from whom Maillol bought it back thirty years later. Introduced to Maillol by Vuillard, Princess Bibesco commissioned two tapestries, *Women's Concert* and *Music for a Bored Princess.* The latter was hung at the Salon, where it attracted a good deal of notice and brought Maillol into the public eye for the first time in his life. With the money from the sale of these works, Maillol, who enjoyed tapestry-making and wanted to continue working at this art, was able to acquire a high warp loom. Unfortunately, the strain to his eyes brought on by weaving nearly ruined his eyesight, and he was obliged to give up his tapestrywork.

The interest in mural decoration was by no means limited to the Nabis. Indeed it was something very much in the air in Europe during the last decade of the nineteenth century. The French decorator Guimard and the Belgian Van de Velde designed furniture and gypsum decorations in the style of *fin de siècle* architecture. In England, Burne-Jones and William Morris drew tapestry cartoons. Maillol shared the enthusiasms of his generation. He too was interested in making objets d'art, though he was soon to take up sculpture.

Notes

[1] Dr. Bassères, *Maillol mon ami*, Perpignan, 1979.
[2] Judith Cladel, *Maillol*, Paris, Grasset, 1937, p. 34.
[3] Octave Mirbeau, *Combats esthétiques*, vol. 2, Paris, Seiguier, 1983, p. 378.
[4] Exhibition catalogue, *Le chemin de Gauguin, genèse et rayonnement*, Saint-Germain-en-Laye, Musée départemental du Prieuré (3rd edition, 1986).
[5] Maurice Denis, "Maillol", *L'Occident*, No. 48, 1905, pp. 241-242.
[6] Judith Cladel, *op. cit.*, p. 53.
[7] *Ibid.*, p. 53.

The Enchanted Garden, ca. 1895
Petit point tapestry
190 x 105 cm

31

Chapter II

The first large sculptures

Maillol's beginnings in sculpture were paradoxically modest. As a student at the Beaux-Arts, he regularly attended drawing and modelling classes. Years of hard work had given him a solid background in the techniques and practice of modelling. In class he worked at building up sculptures "the way you build up a jug." Actually, he made his first sculptures in wood, carving directly into the material – a technique about which he knew almost nothing. "Direct carving is a source of joy to the artist but also a source of difficulty and defeat. Straightaway, starting with a rough sketch, which is all he needs to define his idea, the sculptor frees a head or figure from the block."[1]

Maillol carved his first sculptures in chunks of pear or olive wood in his Banyuls tapestry-making workshop while the girls he employed were busy weaving. "I got the idea of carving a sculpture from a block of wood someone had given me. I traced a circle for the head, another for each shoulder, two more for the breasts, and one for the belly. I was working on this support and managed to carve a woman. She seemed beautiful to me and I was quite pleased with her. The inspiration was there; I had become a sculptor!"[2]

One of the first works to take shape under his skillful fingers was the *Woman with Mandolin*. It is a characteristic example of the style and forms his imagination produced. Its subject is derived from a detail in one of his tapestries, and indeed it has the feeling – the atmosphere of gentle harmony – of his woven work, but transposed to a delicate wood relief. At one level, then, it is about the transition from one medium to another. The female body already appears as an endless source of inspiration to the artist. Like Maillol's other early carved figures, its stylistic qualities reflect a preoccupation with representing temporal values.

The figures in the sculptures from these early years (1895-1896) are often clothed, the artist having no model to pose in the nude. It was only after his marriage to Clotilde Narcisse that the theme of the nude began to appear in his work. *The Source* is probably a tribute to the beauty of her physique. This high-relief in wood reveals the ideals of what was still an art in the making. It is the first example of the characteristic feminine type of Maillol's mature work. The stance of this nude recalls Jean Goujon's nymph on the Fontaine des Innocents in Paris. Maillol is in fact resurrecting an ancient

La Méditerranée, detail, 1905 – Bronze – Paris, Tuileries Gardens

Woman with Mandolin, 1895
Wood
24 x 22 cm

theme: the woman bearing water, that life-giving element. By doing away with all her traditional attributes, such as the amphora or vase, he turns her very body into a source. This eschewal of any distinctive emblem clearly reveals the artist's determination to avoid the literary or symbolic idioms traditionally associated with sculpture.

With *The Source* we come to the issue of the influences that may have shaped the artist's inspiration. One thinks automatically of Gauguin who, after his early sojourns in Brittany and Polynesia, had already carved a large number of sculptures. Gauguin's ideas undeniably made a decisive impact on Maillol in the years when he was searching for his own personal style in painting. Yet Maillol, who was always ready to acknowledge the important role Gauguin played in his life and art – the two were always closely connected – denied that the older artist had any influence on his sculpture. "It has been said that when I began my career I was very influenced by his wood sculptures. That's a myth; he was very useful to me, but only in painting."[3] Like Gauguin, Maillol was interested in primitive art (the discovery of which would soon enable modern art as a whole to reinvent itself in the first years of the

The Source, 1898
Wood
H. 35 cm

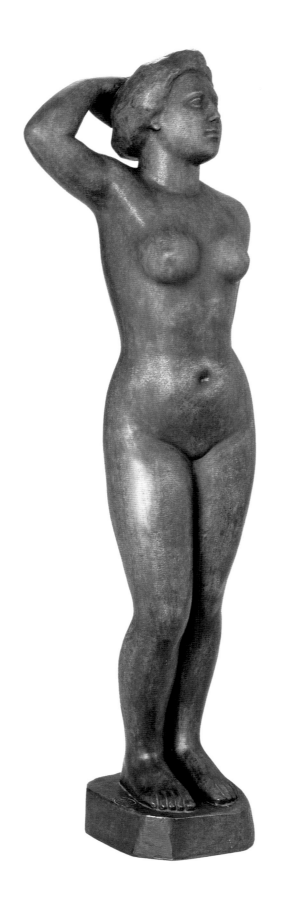

twentieth century), but never permitted it to have a direct influence on his sculpture, which was, as he put it, less "savage."

He admired and studied the Khmer sculptures on display at the Universal Expositions of 1889 and 1900, and was fascinated by ancient Egyptian art with its rigid renderings of the human body. Unlike Gauguin, he did not reject ancient Greek art as a whole. Though he too despised naturalism in art, he had a deep appreciation for archaic sculpture and an unqualified admiration for the work of Phidias. Archaic sculpture was a form of primitivism which allowed him to invent his own concept of sculpture.

As a consequence of an eye inflammation brought on by overwork, Maillol was obliged to give up tapestry. By 1898, sculpture was clearly absorbing all of his energies. He struck out in several directions at once, first working on clothed figures, then on nudes. He did a nude version of the 1899 *Bather*; then, extending his researches, he used the same standing figure for the *Nude Bather* of 1900. With its raised right arm, this figure exemplifies Maillol's fascination with the idea of unveiling the female body, of moving beyond rendering drapery to rendering pure proportions. He continued his exploration of the female body, making it the central theme of his œuvre. While clothes were a link to historicity,

Nude Bather, 1900
Bronze
H. 80 cm

Washerwoman, 1896
Bronze
12 x 28 x 19 cm

changing tastes in fashion, specific periods, the nude seemed to point the way to a timelessness beyond historical references. Maillol began to study the whole range of the human body's positions and gestures: starting with standing figures and then moving on to seated, crouching, recumbent bodies, he tested each position from one sculpture to the next. Before long he was creating masterpieces of balance and perfection. His production was rarely again to attain the intensity it had in this dazzling, deeply moving moment in the genesis of his œuvre.

Within three years he had found the register of forms that he was then to deepen, transform, and expand. Between one sculpture and the next there were constant interactions. Thus one can compare the 1899 *Torso* with another torso sculpted that same year (which has a twisting

movement and out-thrust hip) and with yet a third figure, *Eve Holding the Apple*, which is clearly the most accomplished expression of this series of experiments and is remarkable for the way it combines classical sobriety with a very clean treatment of the figure. *Woman Covering her Breast*, another sculpture of this period, expresses a similar contrast. A female figure struggling to dominate her own sensations, she belongs to a genre in which the dominant feeling is restraint. A space in which time is

Woman Covering Her Breast (La Pudique), 1900
Bronze
17 x 23.5 x 7.5 cm

suspended is present in all of these sculptures. The body and limbs are in harmony with the invisible lines that govern the choice of composition. They seem alive, yet express themselves strictly through slow, mysterious gestures. This description fits most of Maillol's work, especially the series of *Bathers* who seem struck motionless by some supremely imperious message.

Breaking with the classical tradition in sculpture, Maillol blazed a trail in the art of sculpting, one that was radically different from anything that had preceded it. Late nineteenth-century sculpture was a dying art. In spite of the influence of Rodin's genius, academicism still held the field and sculpture was increasingly intent on transcribing literature into stone. Inspiration was being stiffled by a sterile realism combined with an excessive, and excessively literal, reliance on mythological themes.

The degeneration of sculpture seemed in proportion to the staggering proliferation of monuments being erected in every French city and town. Academic wielders of the hammer and chisel were submitting their works by the thousands to the official salons where the bourgeoisie of the Second Empire and the Third Republic applauded the virtuosity of their renderings of bourgeois morality. Maillol sent his first works to the Salon des Artistes Français and the

Eve Holding the Apple, 1899
Bronze
H. 58 cm

Salon of the Société Nationale des Beaux-Arts, where he exhibited (a bas-relief of *Woman Bathing*) for the first time in 1903. However, it was in the recently established Salon d'Automne that he showed his most interesting work.

The rising generation of sculptors to which Maillol belonged, which included Joseph Bernard, Charles Despiau, and Antoine Bourdelle, was united by a common desire to revolutionize the art of sculpture. All of these young artists had worked in Rodin's studio as roughers-out to the ageing master – all of them except Maillol, who consequently felt no need to distance himself from the influence of the sculptor of *The Thinker.* Thus he was able, through the limpid simplicity of his forms, to forge a new style as early as 1905.

Maillol's art is entirely dominated by the geometrical construction of the human body and by a type of beauty that draws its synthetic character from architectural laws. The gist of his sculpture lies in the architectonic construction of the body. In the Spring of 1900, single-mindedly pursuing this idea, he sculpted the plaster figure known as *Recumbent Nude*, a larger version of a statuette he had modelled earlier. He had prepared the mold with the help of Henri Matisse, who was to be a lifelong friend. In much the same way that Matisse was to reduce drawing to line, Maillol was attempting

to reinvent modern sculpture by simplifying forms. In five years of hard work, he achieved this revolution with a series of sculptures entitled *Statue for a Shady Garden, Thought (La Pensée), Latin Thought (La Pensée latine)*, and finally *La Méditerranée.* (All of these titles were given by friends like André Gide, Octave Mirbeau, Paul Lafargue.) *La Méditerranée* represents a woman seated in an attitude of concentration.

Torso with Chemise, 1900
Bronze
H. 21 cm

Thought (La Pensée), 1902-1905 – Bronze – H. 19 cm

41

Her body occupies a neat square; the volumes are so perfectly balanced that she could be described as an abstract construction of an idealized woman absorbed in thought. Shortly before starting work on this figure, Maillol did his first larger than life-size sculpture. It represented a draped female figure seated with one leg folded underneath her. Known under a variety of titles – *Nymph, Flora, Serenity* – it was carved in stone. It was exhibited in Düsseldorf, but was destroyed by an allied bomb in the last months of World War II.

The subject of *La Méditerranée* was one that was already present in Maillol's work. It was first expressed in the relief *The Wave,* and there are other versions of it in the sculptor's painting, drawing, and tapestry-work. In fact, it is one of the abiding themes of his œuvre and it reappears frequently in his experiments. Year after year, Maillol strove to give a concrete shape to his concept of it, first in drawing and painting, then in tapestry, then in sculpture. He made several early versions of *La Méditerranée*, two of which have survived. The first,

La Méditerranée, 1902
Terracotta
16.5 x 19.5 cm

The Wave, 1896 – Bronze – 93 x 103 cm

Recumbent Nude, 1903
Bronze
99 x 103 cm

executed some time between 1900 and 1902, repeats the gesture of the 1896 relief, *The Wave*. This figure's attitude is far more natural than is that of the definitive version of 1905, which is probably the reason why Maillol did not retain it. Though his wife modelled for it, he did not want the finished sculpture to contain any element of resemblance or imitation of reality. One is reminded of Kandinsky's fear that he might unwittingly introduce recognizable shapes, that could be identified as natural signs, into his abstract improvisations.

Maillol wanted something more vigorous and structured. He wanted a formal sobriety that would abolish the anecdotal meaning of physical gestures. What interested him was an absolute – the absolute which was the goal of all his experiments – and not merely sculpting sensual descriptions of the female anatomy.

The numerous studies for *La Méditerranée* clearly reveal the will to simplify that guided Maillol's hand, just as they display the richness of his thought. The preliminary drawings, the tapestry, and the sculpture entitled *Crouching Girl with Chignon,* (1900) all recall the Nabis'

Study for La Méditerranée, 1902
Bronze
17 x 20 cm

influence and the sculptor's interest in Art Nouveau. The relief version of *The Wave* has all the sinuousness – from the folds of the wind-blown blouse and the tumbling mass of the figure's hair to the breaking waves – that characterizes the aesthetic of that turn-of-the-century movement. Yet, despite the artist's obvious interest in this aesthetic, he uses it merely to offset the figure's extreme sobriety and to attenuate the simplification of the planes and modelling. Though he clearly drew his inspiration from nature, the forms and volumes of his figures are governed by an altogether abstract concept. The whole series of crouching, recumbent, and seated figures shows Maillol struggling to achieve ever tighter compositions, trying to resolve the problem of the empty space surrounding his figures' limbs. He felt he had to knit together the different parts of the body, to make each one of them fully meaningful within the cubic volume determining the composition. It was as if the space surrounding each subject constantly required a new definition, thus calling forth yet another version of the figure the sculptor was grappling with. "The reason I strive to bring the limbs together is that one enters a sculpture as one enters a house," Maillol explained.

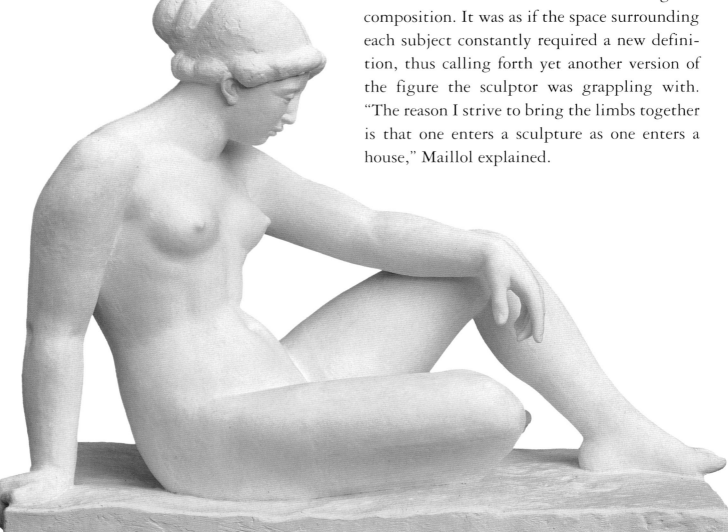

La Méditerranée, 1st version, 1900-1902 – Plaster – 118 x 142 cm

La Méditerranée, 2nd version, 1902-1905 – Bronze – 110 x 120 cm

It was in his native Banyuls that Maillol began to work on translating *Recumbent Woman* (which had hitherto existed only in relief or as a statuette) into a life-size sculpture in the round. In the Spring he had the first version of the sculpture moved to his studio in Marly-le-Roi and continued to work on it there. He could not decide which angle to give to the arm. In sketch after sketch he raised it, bent it at the elbow, sometimes resting it on the knee in a contemplative pose, other times letting it rest on the thigh in a more natural position. The plaster was shown at the Salon d'Automne. In a review of the exhibition, the writer André Gide aptly described in a few phrases the essence of the revolution that Maillol's work was bringing about in the field of sculpture: "In a special room on the ground floor one comes to view several uneven works by Rodin; a few of them are admirable; and all of them seem breathless, anxious, meaningful, and full of clamorous pathos. One goes up to the first floor to a smallish room, in the middle of which Monsieur Maillol's large seated woman is to be seen. She is lovely; she doesn't signify a thing. She is a silent work of art. One has to go far back in time, I believe, to find such a complete indifference to any concern foreign to the simple presentation of beauty."[4] Maillol was indeed the first to take the giant step into modern art, considering the art work as an end in itself. Gide was not wrong to call Maillol the inventor of silence in sculpture. As another writer, Claude Roy, was later to say, "Rodin invented a speechless universe filled with a thousand shouts, and the wordless mouths of the creatures he gave birth to will never stop gasping their unappeasable wail of woe throughout time. Maillol opens the gates of an orchard's realm of silence where shrilling cicadas and murmuring springs weave their torpid terror round Eve and invisible Adam."[5] The work has no message other than its inwardness. Maillol heralds Brancusi's radically simplified volumes and Henry Moore's dislocations.

La Méditerranée and its Olympian calm may indeed have been the birth of modern sculpture. A sculpture that has been freed from the turmoil of passions and movement can surely be said to contain the seeds of an art that is abstract by nature. Twentieth-century art, which was soon to establish abstraction as a major genre, owes its existence first of all to a radical break with the nineteenth century and with neoclassicism. Just as a knowledge of Rodin's art is necessary if one is to understand the movement which swept late nineteenth-century sculpture, it is impossible to dissociate the birth of abstraction from the radical transformation that early twentieth-century sculpture owes to Maillol. A sculpture of motionlessness and inwardness, *La Méditerranée* (though it has nothing literary about it) seems a perfect expression of Baudelaire's intuition in the following lines:

I am as beautiful, O mortals, as a dream in stone,
And my breast, against which each one of you
Has bruised himself, inspires the poet
With eternal love as silent as matter.

I reign in heaven like a sphinx misconstrued;
I am as white as a swan and my heart is like
snow;
I abominate movement which shifts lines from
their place,
And you never hear me weep, never hear me
laugh.[6]

In *La Méditerranée*, Maillol broke with the influences that had connected him with the decorative art of the turn of the century and created a timeless work that is modern before modernity, ancient long after Antiquity. Appropriately enough, the Salon where it was

Nymph, 1900
Bronze
10.5 x 13.5 cm

first shown also marked the advent of Fauvism, not to mention other assaults on official art and academicism, such as the riot of color in the paintings of Derain and Matisse. 1905 was in fact a revolutionary year in art: just as Maillol changed the course of sculpture with *La Méditerranée,* Matisse renewed painting with his submissions to the Salon d'Automne (which, thanks to him and his fellow Fauve painters, has gone down in history as the "Salon des Fauves").

Installed in front of a painting by the Douanier Rousseau, the plaster version of *La Méditerranée* caught the attention of a young German aristocrat and art-lover, who was so taken by it that he commissioned the sculptor to execute it in stone. Count Harry Kessler was to become Maillol's patron and friend. A member of the German aristocracy and a diplomat, he was a great humanist and connoisseur of art and literature. He owned a publishing firm, the "Cranach Presse," and was later to commission the sculptor to illustrate some of the books he produced there.

Count Kessler bought a number of works from Maillol and helped to build the sculptor's reputation in Germany and England. Maillol was by now gradually emerging from poverty and was beginning to make a name for himself.

Writers, art critics, and painters had begun to talk about him; all of them sought to analyze

Small Half-Clothed Flora, 1907
Bronze
H. 65.5 cm

Girl Kneeling, 1900
Bronze
H. 20 cm

the aesthetic qualities that characterize all of his works. Maurice Denis defined the "ingenuousness" of his first sculptures as the proof of his sincerity: "I use the word gaucherie for that type of clumsy declaration which translates the artist's private feelings into something other than conventional expressions. It is not just our old masters the Gothic primitives who give us examples of this felicitous naiveté, but also the greatest of the modern artists. This ingenuousness in physical bearing can be compared to the deliberate awkwardnesses in the work of Puvis de Chavannes, Manet, Renoir, and Degas, who were all reacting to the academic decadence of the Second Empire: it is the defence of sincerity assailed by virtuosity."[7]

Maillol had no truck with the affected poses of nineteenth-century sculpture. One of his masterpieces, *Leda*, offers a striking illustration of his attitude toward tradition. The myth of the god who assumes the guise of a swan in order to seduce the beautiful Queen of Sparta has inspired artists throughout history. Leonardo da Vinci, Rosso, Michelangelo, and Géricault (to mention only a few) were all drawn to this theme. Maillol first tackled it by carving a mirror frame in wood, representing Leda and the swan. He did a number of drawings, rendering different aspects of the myth, as if he was uncertain about which one he wanted to sculpt. Eventually he decided to leave out the swan and made a sculpture of a seated woman. The only reference to the violence of the myth is the gesture of her raised hand repelling the god's advances with deep shame. There are in fact no overt allusions at all to the myth, which has been pared down to the delicate pose of a young girl leaning forward slightly to push back the ardor of an invisible god. This is one of Maillol's most accomplished turn-of-the-century sculptures. The writer Octave Mirbeau, who bought this statuette, recalls that Rodin, who had come to visit him at his home, gazed at it for a long time and then declared, "Maillol is as great as the greatest sculptors. In that little bronze, you see, he sets an example for everyone, the old master as well as the young neophyte. (…) What's admirable about Maillol, and I'll even say what is eternal about him, is the purity, the luminousness, the transparency of his technique and thought."[8] Within a few years, then, the artist of *La Méditerranée* had not only come into his own as a sculptor, but had begun to usher in one of the greatest changes in the history of sculpture. With a few other great artists of the turn of the century, he was inventing modern art.

Notes

[1] Judith Cladel, *Maillol*, Paris, Grasset, 1937, p. 153.
[2] Pierre Camo, *Maillol mon ami*, Lausanne, Éd. du Grand-Chêne, 1950, p. 65.
[3] Judith Cladel, *op. cit.*, p. 39.
[4] André Gide, "Promenade au Salon d'Automne," *Gazette des Beaux-Arts*, December 1, 1905, p. 476.
[5] Claude Roy, *Maillol vivant*, Geneva 1947, p. 33.
[6] Charles Baudelaire, "La Beauté" in *Les Fleurs du Mal*, Paris, Gallimard, 1901, p. 20.
[7] Maurice Denis, in *Le Ciel et l'Arcadie*, coll. Savoir, Paris, Hermann, 1993, p. 109.
[8] Octave Mirbeau, *op. cit.*, p. 380.

Leda, 1900 – Bronze – H. 29 cm

CHAPTER III

Achieving mastery
1905-1914

In the course of the year 1905, Maillol was asked to sculpt a monument to the revolutionary hero Auguste Blanqui. A committee presided over by Blanqui's biographer Gustave Geffroy had been formed for the purpose of honoring Blanqui's memory. The son of one of the revolutionaries who had voted the execution of Louis XVI, Blanqui had inherited his father's radical sentiments and had militated against nearly every French régime in the nineteenth century, from Charles X and Louis-Philippe to Napoleon III. Forever plotting against the bourgeois order, he had spent some thirty-six years in jail, and had died in 1881. His coffin had been accompanied to the grave by a huge crowd waving red flags. The sculptor Dalou's masterpiece, a statue of Blanqui lying dead under his winding sheet, had been erected over the grave.

At Rodin's suggestion, Gustave Geffroy had mobilized such well-known figures as Anatole France, Jean Jaurès, and Octave Mirbeau. He wanted initially to commission Camille

Action in Chains, 1905
Bronze
H. 215.5 cm

Claudel to do the monument, but she was already suffering from the first symptoms of the mental illness that was soon to bring her career to a wretched end. Instead Mirbeau suggested Maillol. The committee agreed and on July 10, 1905, several of its members met with Georges Clemenceau to discuss the project. Maillol, who was later granted an interview with Clemenceau, was deeply impressed by the old man whose indomitable will was to save France in World War I. "He was magnificent," he was to tell Judith Cladel; "his head seemed made of steel. It was as solid as a battleship. By the time I took leave of him, I knew it by heart. I would have sculpted it, not as a portrait, but as a synthesis; it had an admirable structure. It was a rock of power. I never had the opportunity to sculpt it, though, and it is one of my regrets."[1] Maillol started by asking Clemenceau to tell him something about Blanqui and his life. Clemenceau launched into an hour long account of Blanqui's revolutionary career and the numerous years he had spent in prison for his ideals, at the end of which he asked the sculptor what his idea was for the monument. "I'll make you a nice big woman's ass and I'll call it *Liberty in Chains*." Delighted with this

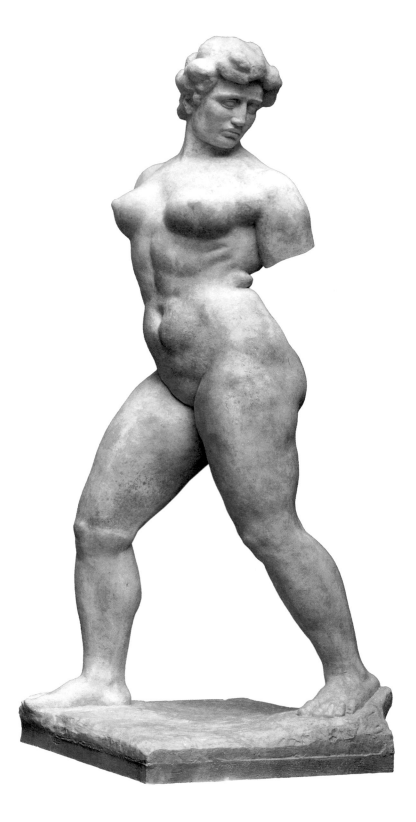

reply, Clemenceau immediately presented him with the seven thousand francs the committee had succeeded in collecting. This amount turned out to be woefully insufficient to cover the cost of making the monument, and Maillol was obliged to pay out of his own pocket for having a mold prepared and the statue cast.

He set to work at once, conceiving the monument as a monumental sculpture of larger than life-size proportions. He wanted to create a figure that would be very large and powerful and – unusually for his work – full of tension. Drawing his inspiration from the biography of Blanqui, he imagined what he felt was a fitting symbol for a life spent mostly behind prison bars. It would be a standing figure, he decided, with one hip thrust out, as if straining to free itself from its bonds.

Action in Chains is full of movement. A striking image of a figure being forcibly restrained, it substitutes anger and a repressed rebelliousness for the characteristic contemplative serenity we usually associate with Maillol. Like *La Méditerranée*, the final version of the monument to Blanqui (also known as *Action in Chains*) was preceded by early variations on the same theme. Maillol sculpted three small sketches and two versions of a large armless torso (one of which, a mold he prepared with Matisse's help, disintegrated), both executed in a mere ten days. He completed the modelling

Armless version of Action in Chains, 1905
Original plaster
H. 220 cm

Torso of Action in Chains, 1905
Bronze
H. 130 cm

of the final version in 1905. A photograph of this clay figure, taken by Octave Mirbeau in the sculptor's studio, can be seen on page 61.

Matisse, who had already helped Maillol make the mold of *La Méditerranée* and was living at this time in the fishing village of Collioure, near Banyuls, would come over to his friend's studio and, every time the sculptor was called away, would moisten the clay of the figure Maillol was shaping. One morning, as Matisse was dampening the cloth swaddling the clay, the sculpture collapsed. This was the first "state" of the armless version. Maillol promptly set to work again and sculpted a second armless torso directly in plaster. He settled on the final version after making dozens of sketches, studies, and drawings. Remarkably, in spite of their small size all of the studies and statuettes have a monumental character and retain their miraculous balance and freshness even when transferred to a large scale. *Action in Chains* is one of Maillol's few sculptures expressing movement. Though at first glance it suggests a certain tension between its different volumes, essentially it renders movement through its structure. The balanced composition and strangely calm power of the monument to Auguste Blanqui give it a feeling of intimacy despite its massiveness, a tenderness in its *terribilità*. For everything in this sculpture rests on the contrast between massive

Study for Action in Chains, 1905
Bronze
H. 33 cm

weight and lightness; the impression one gets is that the sculptor struggled to transform the power of its movement into a gesture at once flowing and fettered.

Maillol, then, seems not to have found it difficult to break away from his static concept of sculpture – at least not when the subject required him to do so. When Rodin first saw *Action in Chains*, a work which came closer to his own form of art than anything Maillol had hitherto sculpted, he remarked enigmatically, "It needs looking at again." Was this criticism, or was it on the contrary praise masquerading as professional understatement? Unfortunately, Rodin never referred to the sculpture again. In October 1908, the monument to Blanqui was erected at Puget-Théniers. It was never officially inaugurated, however, for the public authorities of the time found it disturbed their Third Republic tastes and preferred to ignore its existence. During World War II, the Germans removed a large number of public sculptures from France in order to melt them down for their metal. Worried about the fate of *Action in Chains*, Matisse offered to buy it from the the municipality of Puget-Théniers and donated it to the city of Nice. He envisioned it standing beside the highway from Italy, offering the traveller his first image of France. Cast in bronze, it has now been installed in the Tuileries Gardens in Paris.

In 1907, Maillol exhibited the original plaster version of his sculpture *Desire*, which would later be cast in lead for Count Kessler. *Desire* was to be the first high-relief in a series based

Head of Action in Chains, detail, 1905
Bronze

on the theme of the male-female couple. The sobriety of its construction and geometrical composition is alleviated by the sensuality of the subject. The two figures are perfectly contained within the frame that seems to screen them from the world; their bodies are frozen in an expression that would become familiar in Maillol's œuvre. The woman's hand is raised in a last attempt to restrain the man, to whom she is already surrendering. The sculpture was a sensation. Emile Bernard declared that by itself it justified holding the Salon that year. Raymond Duchamp-Villon borrowed its composition for his own relief of lovers, which he sculpted in homage to Maillol. Yet increasingly the latter's art with its timeless ideal of beauty, was distancing itself from the other currents of modern sculpture emerging around this time.

For this was the period in which Picasso was working on his first *art nègre* sculptures. The painted wood carving of 1907, *Standing Man*, was already clearly stamped with the African character that the Spanish artist would seek to give his sculpture up until 1908, thereby sharing Maillol's concern (evident in his *Bathers*, for example) with inventing a synthetic art that would transcend accidental particulars and express universal traits. In her book on Picasso, Gertrude Stein suggests that it was in fact Maillol who first became interested in African masks. Although he never used African art the way Picasso did, he admired its power and richness of expression. Morever, the large Gauguin retrospective of 1906 profoundly influenced all those artists who were not as yet thoroughly familiar with his work (which was not Maillol's case). In Derain's early works, like his *Crouching Woman* of 1907, and in Matisse's *Reclining Nude* of the same year, the presence of Gauguin's influence is manifest, as is that of primitivism and modernism.

This interest in primitivism freed the artistic imagination from the conventions of representation. At the same time, by liberating the art work from set ideas about what is considered proper or seemly, it ushered in an inner vision of art. Maillol's ideal of a pure sculpture based on the body's architecture and on a harmony between volumes got him unfairly catalogued as a neoclassicist. This misapprehension obviously springs from the impression of legibility that his sculptures, like the masterpieces of archaic Greek sculpture which he admired so deeply, offer to the viewer. Yet Maillol never considered repeating the lesson of the Greeks. His sculpture was entirely his own invention, and if it can be compared to the great works of Antiquity, this is solely thanks to its power and to the freshness of its inspiration.

For that matter, can one really reduce Picasso's sculpture to a simple transfer of African art to modern art? To be sure, the discovery of the indigenous arts of Africa and the South Pacific made the invention of Cubism possible, but in fact what modern art brought was a concept of art in which the artist's imagination has unlimited power. Aspiring to the absolute expression of volume in and of itself, Maillol's work embodied this spirit as early as the turn of the century.

As it happens, Maillol soon had an opportunity to compare his personal inspiration with that of the ancient Greek sculptors, whose works he was as yet only very slightly familiar with. Count Kessler invited him to join him on a trip to Greece with another companion, the poet Hugo von Hofmannsthal. Maillol was reluctant at first, but finally accepted his patron's offer. The thought of being able to view the ancient Greek sculptures in their native setting was too much to resist, and, in the Spring of

Clay of Action in Chains
Photographed by Octave Mirbeau
in Maillol's studio, 1905

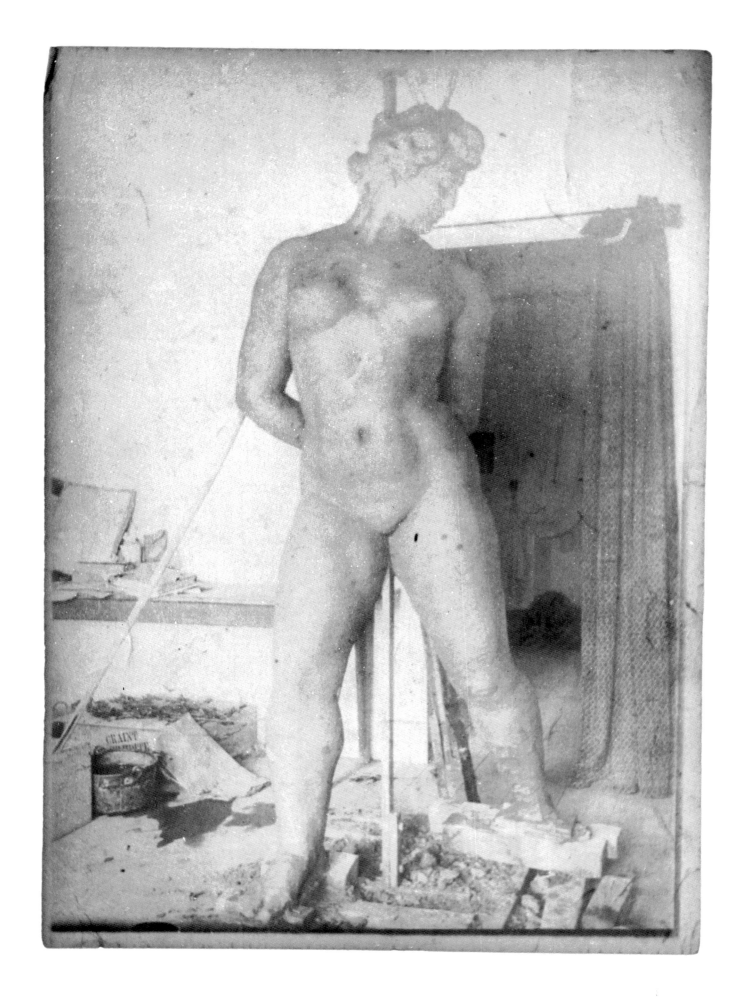

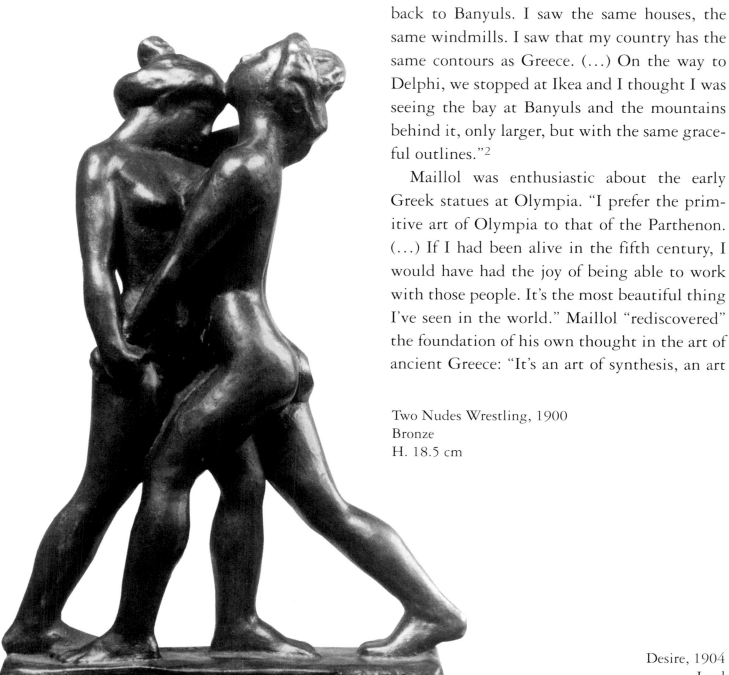

1908, he met Count Kessler in Marseilles. His first glimpse of Piraeus and its bay was a real shock to him: the Greek landscape reminded him powerfully of the country around Banyuls. "Arriving in Greece, I thought I was coming back to Banyuls. I saw the same houses, the same windmills. I saw that my country has the same contours as Greece. (…) On the way to Delphi, we stopped at Ikea and I thought I was seeing the bay at Banyuls and the mountains behind it, only larger, but with the same graceful outlines."[2]

Maillol was enthusiastic about the early Greek statues at Olympia. "I prefer the primitive art of Olympia to that of the Parthenon. (…) If I had been alive in the fifth century, I would have had the joy of being able to work with those people. It's the most beautiful thing I've seen in the world." Maillol "rediscovered" the foundation of his own thought in the art of ancient Greece: "It's an art of synthesis, an art

Two Nudes Wrestling, 1900
Bronze
H. 18.5 cm

Desire, 1904
Lead
H. 120 cm

that is superior to the the labor of the flesh that we moderns are searching for."[3]

Unlike Greek sculpture, Maillol's work sought to capture a beauty that expressed, rather than an idealization of the human body, a synthesis of the artist's perception of loveliness and a representation that encompassed his view of the world. The first to express a sensation of the body in all its immediacy as a thing that is beautiful in itself and not as an idealization of beauty, Maillol saw no point in imitating antique models.

The Cyclist is a case in point. Apart from the reliefs, it is one of the few masculine sculptures in Maillol's œuvre. At Count Kessler's request, Maillol sculpted a nude, the model for which was a young automobile racer named Auguste Colin. His anatomy had a dry, nervy leanness which had struck the sculptor's imagination. The polar opposite of a sculpture like *The Bathers*, *The Cyclist* has a tense vitality that recalls Rodin's work. Seeing it exhibited at the Salon d'Automne in 1909, the latter exclaimed, "I didn't think you were capable of this."[4]

The Cyclist exemplifies Maillol's experimental approach to rendering flesh: though

Armless version of The Cyclist, 1907
Bronze
H. 98.5 cm

Phrynée, 1910
Bronze
H. 41 cm

The Cyclist, 1907
Bronze
H. 98.5 cm

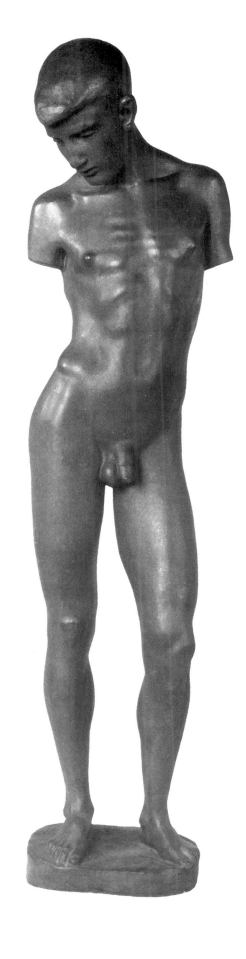

inspired by a specific body, it presents us with a synthetic, if not abstract, view of the male anatomy. Avoiding any dramatization of the subject, the modelling expresses a strange quietness which is rendered with such perfect simplicity that it achieves Maillol's ideal of sculpture purely articulating the human fact as an idiom of creation. Maillol and Count Kessler returned to France after spending a month in

Night, 1902
Bronze
H. 18 cm

Greece, buoyed with the feeling that they had visited the land of happiness, "the fatherland of artists." Maillol brought back two or three blocks of Greek marble, which he intended to use for future sculptures. His need to create was stronger than ever and his courage and will to work had both been enormously strengthened by his travels in the landscapes of Antiquity. The following year, he completed a sculpture he had been working on for many years. Entitled *Night*, this self-enclosed statue is an emblem of repose, serenity, and impassivity. Because of its utter sobriety and rounded volumes, it has often been compared to the cube-shaped statues of ancient Egypt. Entering it in the Salon of the Société Nationale des Artistes Français, Maillol had it installed right in the middle of the rotunda of the Grand Palais in Paris. The day before the opening Rodin, who was in charge of the sculpture section, gave instructions for one of his own works to be displayed on the same spot. On learning that it was already taken, he declared loftily, "Leave Maillol's figure where it is."[5] The next day, he went to examine *Night* and remarked, "One forgets too often that the human body is an architecture – a living architecture." Though the two sculptors had very different ideas about form, they clearly understood each other and experienced the art of sculpture with the same intensity.

Woman and Dove, 1905
Bronze
H. 25.4 cm

Maillol's constant goal was to create figures that stand out in space, but remain closely connected with the material out of which they are shaped. "I strive for architecture and volumes," he once observed. "Sculpture is architecture, a balancing of masses, a tasteful composition. It is difficult to attain this architectural aspect. I try to render it the way Polycletes succeeded in rendering it. My point of departure is always a geometrical figure — a square, a rhomb, a triangle, since they are the figures that are most stable in space."[6] One is reminded of Cézanne's famous precept about painting. Maillol replaced narrative sculpture with human forms enclosed within geometrical figures. He labored to express the diversity of organic beings, but reduced their manifoldness to a simplified formula that prefigured abstraction. The next stage was to be reached when Brancusi, declaring that it was no longer necessary to render hollows and shadows in sculpture, would push the geometrical treatment of forms to a complete paring down of volumes and move one step further away from tangible images of reality. Little by little, the human image was to lose its cohesion as the creators of modern art were to free themselves from their dependence on the strictures of reality.

For his part, Maillol struggled tirelessly to express his view of sculpture by concentrating on the almost impossible task of

Night, 1st version, 1902
Bronze
H. 118 cm

Night, 1907-1909
Bronze
H. 106 cm

simultaneously expressing all forms in one while giving to the body's presence the infinite power which it contains. *La Méditerranée* revealed Maillol's existence to the small world of art connoisseurs. His first public acclaim came when his sculpture *Pomona* was exhibited at the Salon d'Automne in 1910. A celebration of restrained power, of sensuality stripped of mere prettiness, this figure is a vigorous expression of a serene, primordial beauty.

Pomona portrays a female type very different from that of Maillol's other works, though it could be compared to the 1898 relief *The Source*. (And the proportions of that figure in profile are reminiscent of those of the 1910 *Pomona*). Notwithstanding the fact that he claimed he never copied from nature, Maillol used a model for the latter, one of his major works. Her name was Laure. "I used her," the sculptor admitted, "but I invented her. I used her simply as a crutch." He sometimes employed models for his sketches, rarely for his sculpture; though he would reproduce their figures literally in drawing, he avoided doing so when carving or modelling.

It seems, in fact, that the actual presence of a model distracted him from the idea he was seeking to express. His initial concept for a sculpture would come from a figure, a pose, an attitude he visualized in his mind, but never from an actual model. He used models merely as a way of clarifying and testing his ideas. He wanted at all costs to avoid any suggestions of actual physical traits. "I am not interested in particulars," he said; "what interests me is the general idea. What captivates you in Michelangelo, who is so far removed from Egyptian art, is the idea of power, the overall concept, the task he has set himself." [7]

Pomona is one of Maillol's major works. A virtual manifesto of his art, it attains a degree of compactness, a density unprecedented in the history of sculpture. A symbol of fertility, the statue seems inhabited by the dark forces of some primitive art; as an emblem of the female body, it harks back to the earliest mother-divinities, yet transforms them in the light of a new aesthetic, a purified concept of volumes.

The statue's artistic success is as great as were the reactions of scorn and disgust expressed by the first critics to review it. Yet even they were unable to prevail against its calm power. Maillol, whose work had hitherto met mostly with hostility and indignation, got his first taste of fame with *Pomona*. His name was on every lip in artistic circles, and his reputation abroad was definitely launched.

One of the visitors at the Salon of 1910 was a Russian named Ivan Abramovich Morosov. He viewed *Pomona* and was deeply impressed. Ivan Morosov, who had been an amateur painter in his youth, had acquired an extraordinary art collection which included works by such artists as Cézanne, Van Gogh, Renoir, Redon, Vuillard, Bonnard, and Signac. He allowed himself to be guided in his choice of art works

Pomona, 1910
Bronze
H. 164 cm

by a Swiss collector who had a passion like his own for modern art, Mrs. Hahnloser. In 1910, Morosov was one of the most famous art collectors in Europe. He was to lose his collection in the Russian Revolution, though managed to have his home declared a museum and served for a time as a guide showing visitors around his former collection. He not only acquired *Pomona*, but succeeded as well in convincing Maillol to sculpt a series of allegorical figures representing the four seasons.

Maillol had by no means exhausted his source of inspiration for *Pomona*, for he was to return to this figure many times in his career. Meanwhile, he accepted Morosov's sizeable commission and was to spend several years working on it. He decided to stick to his initial idea of using youthful figures to symbolize the seasons. The series, he explained to Judith Cladel, would be "a hymn to youth." He did not use a model for *Flora*, *Spring*, and *Summer* – unlike *Pomona* – and sculpted them entirely from memory. As with his previous works, each figure would go through a number of different stages and would be the triumphant conclusion of a lengthy plastic exploration.

For a pioneer of modernity like Maillol, borrowing the iconography of the eighteenth and nineteenth centuries was of course out of the question. Faithful to his own art, he used the opportunity offered by Morosov's commission

Flora, 1911
Bronze
H. 167 cm

to imagine entirely new figures to satisfy his requirements for harmony and synthesis. As Maurice Denis remarked, Maillol had a gift for condensing and summarizing in a limited number of clear, concise forms the infinitely diversified relationships we observe in nature.

After executing a large number of preliminary drawings, Maillol sculpted several early versions of the seasons, working on each figure's profile, its volumes, the angle of its limbs, the proportions between its different parts, unflaggingly pursuing an idea that seemed to escape him each time he tried to capture it.

Flora, his most famous work after *Pomona*, went through several states. The draped version, which is the one he finally settled on, is characterized by slender forms emerging transparently beneath a long gauzy tunic. The figure's hands hang at her sides, holding an offering of a garland of flowers. There were two versions of this draped *Flora*, but Maillol brought only one of them to completion before casting it in bronze. A clothed torso and a fragment are also known to exist, and in addition to them there are two different nude statues of *Flora*. The same is true of the other seasons.

Spring is a delicate figure, far more slender and youthful than the mature anatomy of *Pomona*. Clearly Maillol enjoyed creating syntheses of very different body types. *Spring* is an

Spring, 1911
Bronze
H. 171 cm

73

almost pubescent female anatomy and its forms are barely suggested. It also exists in an armless version, for which Maillol sculpted two states, later having the one he preferred cast in bronze.

Several versions of *Summer* are known to exist as well, the most famous being an armless and headless *Torso*. The twisting movement of the hips is expressed with a total freedom that seems to bring the torso alive with an undulating movement from top to bottom.

Maillol completed the series of seasons just before the outbreak of World War I. His feeling of isolation and dejection at the sheer scale of the hostilities made it impossible for him to continue working on any of his large-scale projects for the entire duration of the conflict.

Notes
[1] Judith Cladel, *Maillol*, Grasset, Paris, 1937, p. 76.
[2] *Ibid.*, p. 93.
[3] *Ibid.*, p. 97.
[4] *Ibid.*, p. 92.
[5] *Ibid.*, p. 82.
[6] *Ibid.*, p. 148.
[7] *Ibid.*, p. 128.
[8] John Rewald, "Souvenirs de Maillol", in the catalogue for the Maillol exhibition in Japan, 1984, p. 43.

Torso of Spring, 1911
Bronze
H. 85 cm

Summer, 1910-1911
Bronze
H. 162.5 cm

CHAPTER IV

The monumental sculptures

The outbreak of hostilities found Maillol in Marly-le-Roi where he had installed a small paper manufacturing shop next to his house and studio. He was working on the illustrations for Ovid's *Art of Love* which Count Kessler had commissioned. Not satisfied with commercial paper, he had devised and hand manufactured his own paper known as "papier Montval" with his initials and those of his patron in the watermark.

Anticipating the worst, Count Kessler sent Maillol a telegram advising him to bury his statues. In the feverish atmosphere of the war's first days, this nearly cost Maillol his life. He was accused of spying for the enemy and an angry crowd set fire to his paper workshop. Organized by the right-wing writer Léon Daudet, a violent press campaign was unleashed against him, accusing him of treason. The myth of Maillol the German sympathizer was to re-emerge during World War II.

Maillol paid heavily for his friendship with Count Kessler and for his successes in pre-war

Germany. He put a temporary stop to all of his work and lived through the war years in anguish. His son Lucien was mobilized, and the sculptor sank deeper than ever into depression. It seemed to him impossible to carry on creating works based on humanistic values and bearing a message of harmony and joy at a time when mankind was destroying itself. The years dragged by endlessly. In 1917 Rodin died. Maillol was now the only truly great living sculptor of his generation.

It was only with the end of the war and Lucien's safe return that Maillol was able to get back to work. One of the projects he resumed was a monument to Cézanne he had been commissioned to do several years earlier. A committee presided by the founder of the Salon d'Automne, Frantz Jourdain, had been organized to honor the memory of the master from Aix-en-Provence. It included the closest friends of the deceased artist as well as several of Maillol's own friends. Despite a number of generous cash donations, the committee had

Clothed Pomona, detail, 1921
Plaster
H. 174 cm

(Overleaf.) Monument to Cézanne, 1912-1925
Lead
145 x 222 cm

disbanded, unable to decide on a specific project. Maillol's chances of convincing the public authorities to accept one of his works were virtually nil, yet the idea of paying homage to Cézanne meant a great deal to him.

He worked on the monument for years. After making numerous preliminary drawings, he decided it should be a monumental figure capable of organizing the open space surrounding it. "Maillol's happiest moments came with the opportunity he was sometimes given to construct a statue within an architectural or natural setting: the monuments to the war dead in his native South, the state commissions for public parks and buildings... Someone once said that a canvas has to be able to stand on its own in a field of wheat. But the decisive test for Maillol's statues, the one that reveals their secret, is how they withstand the comparison with trees and nature, stones and buildings."[1]

Never before had the concept of architecture played such a vital role in his thought. Several earlier sculptures mark the stages towards the definitive version of the *Monument to Cézanne*. One of the earliest studies for it that we know of is a headless and legless statuette. The position of the body is substantially more upright than in later versions, and its surface bears the marks of the sculptor's hands. Many of Maillol's

Recumbent Nude, 1912
Plaster
17 x 21 cm

first sculpture studies show a good deal of modelling; it is only after months of work, if not years, that the finished sculpture attained the smoothness of a pebble polished by the sea. He made study after study to determine the angle of the head and arms, and in some sketches experimented with draping the figure. In the end, he produced two definitive versions of the monument. The first, completed in 1920, represents a woman of regal bearing reclining on a drapery. Ever since Ripa's iconography, rivers have been personified by similar recumbent figures (moreover water is a familiar allegory of time). The figure's legs are treated in the spirit of Cézanne as geometric volumes. As the writer Jules Romains remarked, Maillol's art is an art of "equilibrium, of going beyond ordinary limits, and also of superb discretion. Nothing in it calls attention to itself. Its essential principles don't seem to feel the need to declare themselves or raise their voice in order to command respect. (…) The composition, harmony, and symmetry of his statues are deliberately unobtrusive. Even when I think of the figure in the *Monument to Cézanne*, I feel that Maillol's sculpture reaches beyond the classical equilibrium to primitivism."[2]

The primitivism Maillol drew on for his statues was not the primitivism that inspired

Recumbent Nude, 1921
Bronze
151 x 248 x 78 cm

Picasso or Brancusi. Maillol's interest in primitive art goes back to his Nabi period and to Gauguin, whose influence was decisive because it showed him a radically new approach to the world of form. He studied the plastic expression of other civilizations, notably ancient Egyptian sculpture whose majesty and tranquillity he admired deeply. At the Universal Exposition of 1900, he discovered Khmer art and, with the permission of the security guards at the Indochinese pavilion, was able to make molds of bas-reliefs from the temple of Angkor. He delighted in Indian art and in the serenity of Buddhist sculpture. Christian Zervos is right to observe that "with other premises and a very different effect, Maillol was a precursor of today's Constructivists. All his figures create an impression of massive structure, of a search for beautiful volumes. They are encompassed by powerful square or pyramidal geometrical forms resting on large surfaces."[3]

His sculpture contains the quietude of a body in perfect balance and invites us to reflect on the meaning of modernity. It constructed a cohesive human figure precisely when modern art was abolishing it. Perhaps it is this that makes it difficult to perceive the meaning of his art, an art which offered a pure, simplified

Sketch for the Port-Vendres
Monument to the War Dead, 1921
Bronze
26 x 36 cm

Port-Vendres Monument to the War Dead, ca. 1923
Lead
168 x 223 cm

view of formal harmony at the very time when modern art was rejecting the qualities of the aesthetic it upheld. The *Monument to Cézanne* was turned down by the city of Aix-en-Provence. Only in 1925 was it eventually acquired by the French state, and installed in the Tuileries Gardens in Paris.

After the war, the state commissioned French artists to design monuments to honor an entire generation of soldiers who had been killed in action. Most of them yielded to bombast and pathos, but Maillol chose a silent image to express the tragedy of a nation's youth being sacrificed in battle. Thus, when the town of Port-Vendres commissioned him to sculpt a monument to the war dead, he returned to the theme of the recumbent female figure he had been working on for several years. He used his studies for the *Monument to Cézanne* as the basis for this new work. Having observed the effect produced by the dampened cloths he wrapped his clay figures in, he decided to mold the

statue first and then work on the folds, in effect using drapery as a way of giving fluidity to volumes. He completed the monument in Port-Vendres. Waiving all payment, he simply asked to be reimbursed for the cost of the materials he had used in making the statue.

These commissions brought others. For the town of Céret, Maillol proposed doing a figure of a seated woman leaning forward slightly in a meditative attitude. Executed between 1921 and 1923, it was called *Grief*. It is part of the series of seated women that began with *La Méditerranée.* As Pierre Camo was later to explain, "Maillol got the idea for the Céret monument from observing his sister-in-law sitting by the fireside."[4]

With extremely simplified means, Maillol translated this idea into a monument to the war dead. "One can express grief with motionless features," he said, "but not with a twisted expression and wide open mouth."[5] He used the theme of *Grief* again a few years later for a funeral monument for the Basel cemetery: another seated female figure, but this time in an erect posture, with her forearm resting on her thigh. She is draped, as if wrapped in the silence of her thoughts.

To understand the genesis of Maillol's statues, one must view his drawings and especially his small sketch books. The drawings map out the progression of his thought and the

Basel Monument, ca. 1935   Grief, 1921
Plaster   Bronze
Studio photograph   155 x 110 cm

Clothed Pomona, 1922
Plaster
H. 174 cm

Elne Monument to the War Dead, ca. 1925 – Stone

Clothed Pomona, 1921 – Bronze – H. 174 cm

Draped Pomona, 1921
Original plaster
176 x 61 x 57 cm

Clothed Pomona, 1921
Bronze
181 x 61 x 48 cm

different stages of his explorations. He never went anywhere without a small sketch book and would often jot down a gesture, an attitude, or movement that caught his eye during one of his walks. The statue he dedicated to the town of Elne belongs to his characteristic register of forms. He derived the theme from *Pomona*, a subject to which he would return again and again. He clothed the figure's ample forms in a flowing dress with regular folds and altered the angle of her arms. Thanks to the understanding mayor, who admired his work, Maillol was able to erect his statue on a terrace, close to a group of olive trees, in the middle of a landscape of vineyards and gardens between the sea and a line of blue hills. The choice of an appropriate location for his work gave enormous pleasure to Maillol, who felt that a

sculpture's siting was a decisive factor in the viewer's perception of its beauty.

There is one exception to the series of monuments which Maillol sculpted between the two wars. To honor his birthplace, the sculptor executed a three-part high-relief in Banyuls. It is unlike anything else in his œuvre. He chose an admirable location for it, a promontory above the port which was an ideal spot for contemplation and meditation. Looking out over the bay, the monument greets the traveller arriving by sea. Maillol claimed proudly that "No ancient monument was ever erected in front of such a beautiful landscape. Look at the sea, you could eat it up with your eyes! You've got to view the monument with the sea, you understand, the line of the horizon. That's why I made it. I wanted to create stones on the sea.

Banyuls Monument to the War Dead, 1930-1932
Bronze

It's an architectural composition rather than a sculpture."[6] In another letter addressed to Pierre Camo, he wrote, "I have at least made something which satisfies me. Sculpture on a rock in the middle of the sea – quite simply three things, the sky, the sea, and a carved stone. I added the grievous feeling of war as I experienced it. I would have preferred doing a hymn to joy; instead I will have left an idea of sorrow on that rock at Banyuls which I will have linked to the sun, the sea, and the landscape, which is so beautiful in that place."[7]

What strikes one first about the Banyuls monument is the geometry of the composition, then its architectural aspect, then the vastness of the sea. Here again Maillol strove to escape the contingent and the particular and to attain the absolute. He condensed human suffering in an expression of poignant sobriety. In the account of one contemporary, Henri Frère: "We entered the studio to view the bas-relief he was working on. It was the monument's left-hand relief, *The Wife and the Mother*. 'I wanted to charge it with human feeling. The woman is inconsolable and the old lady is holding back her tears, you see. That's human. (…) I did away with all details. The figure mustn't be a woman of flesh and blood. When doing this sort of thing, one has to place oneself outside of time. It's got to be eternal.' He showed me too how the composition fitted into the rectangle

Torso of Île-de-France, 1921
Bronze
H. 120 cm

Île-de-France, 1925
Bronze
H. 167 cm

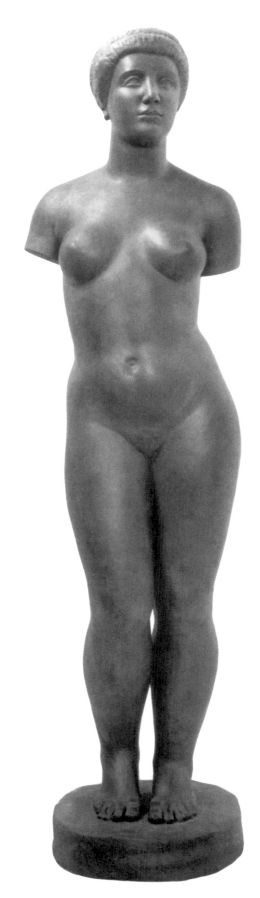

Armless Bather, front and back, 1921
Bronze
92　H. 170 cm

Draped Bather, or The Seine, 1921
Bronze
H. 175 cm

Nude Bather, 1921
Bronze
H. 170 cm

and how the lines were balanced, and added, 'It has to be calm. (…) I eliminated the children because they crowded the composition, just as I eliminated all the details of the old woman's clothes. One must always simplify, get rid of everything that doesn't contribute to feeling in order to give one's work amplitude and spaciousness.'"[8] Completed in 1932, the Banyuls monument to the war dead is the only one of Maillol's works to be based on the traditional iconography of funerary art. The sculptor's figures are not connected through multiple

Debussy Torso, 1930
Bronze
H. 81 cm

Monument to Debussy, 1930
Bronze
H. 92 cm

profiles to the space surrounding them; they require a frontal reading and need to be strictly isolated. Thus a statue like *Île-de-France* is structured in terms of a unity of vision paradoxically offering a multiplicity of viewpoints. Yet again, the definitive work was preceded by numerous preliminary versions. It was in fact composed piecemeal. Maillol began by sculpting a torso, which is an art work in itself. He then added a head and limbs. The figure appears to be emerging from a river; its torso is one of the purest in the sculptor's entire œuvre. It is filled with uncharacteristic movement. An artist of stillness, Maillol nevertheless observed that when movement is rendered "with too much emphasis, it becomes frozen; it is no longer life. The immobility that an artist creates is not at all the same as the stillness of photography. An art work contains a latent life, potential movement."[9] A concept that is situated at the antipodes of the Futurist position – especially that of a sculptor like Boccioni who held that representing the reality of movement was crucial.

It was by rejecting expressivity and pathos that Maillol pioneered a revolution in sculpture. At a time when artists were striving to translate increasingly diversified fields into plastic forms (like Kandinsky seeking to render musicality in painting), Maillol's sculpture addressed the issue of art's territory with an entirely different economy. He believed, for example, that there are laws of harmony which apply to sculpture just as there are laws of harmony in music.

In homage to the memory of the composer Debussy, he imagined a kneeling muse, though he had in fact never heard any of the compositions of the author of *L'Après-midi d'un faune*. His favorite composers were Bach, Couperin, Rameau, Mozart; he was fond of jazz and the traditional music of his native region, especially the sardanas of the local fishermen. The monument to Debussy combines harmonious forms with an almost mathematically rigorous composition. Like virtually all of his sculpture, it is built on a counterpoint of silence and breath, space and solid volumes; its rhythms might be those of a Bach composition, and like all music it attempts to give form to thought.

Maillol, whose œuvre includes a large number of torsos, believed that in sculpture the head was only the upper part of the body and must not be given an "expression." Most of his faces are impassive and do not appear to possess any inner life. He did not want to express grief or moral anguish in physiognomic terms. The beauty of his statues does not rest on any accuracy of details, but on a synthesis; he wanted their heads and faces to be as abstract as possible, so as to avoid any suggestion of a particular, contingent expression. He was not interested in making his figures lifelike, but in bringing out their specific harmony – a harmony whose apex was

Bust of Renoir, 1907
Bronze
H. 41 cm

the head conceived not as a portrait but as the final element in a series of proportions.

Nonetheless Maillol did sculpt a few portraits: his wife, his friend Terrus, Odilon Redon's son Harry, Maurice Denis' wife Marthe, Renée Rivière, Auguste Renoir.

At the painter's request, he sculpted a bust of Renoir in 1906. Unfortunately, the clay collapsed after only a few sessions. Nevertheless, encouraged by Renoir, Maillol completed the portrait, which represents the artist wearing his favorite hat. The treatment is firm; the leanness of the face underscores the acuity in the expression of a painter who had devoted his life to capturing the most transient of life's impressions. Inspired by his experience of sitting for Maillol, Renoir decided shortly therereafter to take up sculpture himself, and, by guiding the hand of the sculptor Guino, with whom he worked closely, succeeded in transposing his pictorial forms into three-dimensional figures.

A work like *Venus Genitrix*, with its ample volumes and softly rounded curves, recalls Maillol's sculptures, but one cannot really speak of a reciprocal influence between the two artists. Undeniably, though, there is a certain kinship between their forms. The presence of the portrait and the amplification of specific details confirms the difference between their œuvres, though both are based on a lasting fascination with the beauty of the body and its plastic qualities. "In order to attain beauty of form," Ingres once said, "you've got to model roundly and skip inner details." Maillol seems to have followed this prescription to the letter in sculpting his portraits of Renoir and Terrus. If by "inner details" one means the quiver of desire on lips, the luminousness of an eye, the always fleeting trace of inner motions and emotions, then the faces of Maillol's sculptures are almost never actual faces but rather masks worn by living anatomies. Maillol wanted to crown his statues with an architectural element devoid of any strictly personal meaning, thereby expressing the kind of inner life that the sculptors of the Orient have traditionally been able to embody in their statues.

Notes

[1] Claude Roy, *Maillol vivant*, Geneva, 1947, p. 37.
[2] Jules Romain, *Forme*, No. IV, 1930.
[3] Christian Zervos, "Notes sur la sculpture contemporaine", *Cahiers d'Art*, No. 4, 1929.
[4] Pierre Camo, *Maillol mon ami*, Lausanne, Éd. du Grand-Chêne, 1950.
[5] Judith Cladel, *Maillol*, Paris, Grasset, 1937, p. 135.
[6] Pierre Camo, *op. cit.*
[7] *Ibid.*
[8] H. Frère, *Conversation avec Maillol*, Geneva, P. Cailler, 1956.
[9] Judith Cladel, *op. cit.*, p. 135.

Head of Dina, 1944
Bronze
H. 24.5 cm

99

Chapter V

An intimate, eternal vision of woman (1920-1944)

When fame finally came to Maillol, he was on the threshold of old age, yet the years do not seem to have weighed on his shoulders. A man gifted with more than usual energy and physical stamina, he worked ceaselessly, as if his days were numbered. Toward the end of his life he would go on long tramps in the mountains, where his gaunt erect figure would become a familiar sight. A gourmet, though ever a frugal eater, he was fond of seasoning his dishes with the herbs of his native soil. He almost always wore a long light-brown or beige jacket with a cap or soft hat in matching tones – except in his later years, when he invariably sported a beret. A long untidy beard and piercing steel-blue eyes dominated his features.

Maillol liked to have guests, and the Sunday gatherings at his house in Marly-le-Roi near Paris were famous. He was warm and hospitable and never discouraged young artists from calling on him. The air of dignity that emanated from his presence and the extreme sensitivity of his personality commanded respect.

The Nymph in the Sculptor's Studio, 1930
Plaster
Photo Brassaï

Untroubled by ambitiousness, he was above all a man of taste, cultivated and perceptive. "Maillol did not share the *angst* of his century."[1] At no point did his art ever render the pessimistic outlook that modern art draws on in order to express the nihilism of an age which, marked by the death of the concept of the aesthetic, elevates the dark forces of the unconscious to the rank of new values.

Nonetheless, Maillol took an interest in all the different currents of the art world during his lifetime, though he kept aloof from them and continued to work at pursuing his own private vision. One can base an entire œuvre on a single idea, he liked to repeat.

One of Maillol's achievements is that he created a new perception of the female anatomy. It is interesting to compare him with another artist whose main source of inspiration was the nude: Degas. Degas' art too is infused with a clarity of drawing. The painter relied on his deep understanding of lines to render the physical world. He took his subjects from daily life: dancers, prostitutes, women ironing or putting on their clothes. But in each case he isolated figure from context. What Maillol shares with Degas is an essentially plastic

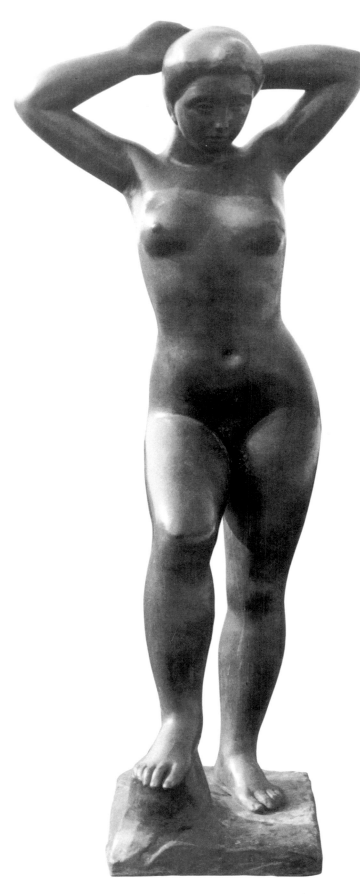

perception of the female body. A dancer's *déhanché* and a bather bending down to grasp her foot bring certain shapes and volumes into play – and this is what interested both artists. Both instinctively sought to represent the female anatomy in its simplest, calmest, most natural postures.

Maillol's sculpture achieves an ideal balance through the accuracy of its proportions as well as the harmoniousness of its compositions. Paul Valéry once said that sculpture is an art full of surprises, and at each moment the sculptor chooses his viewpoint among an infinite array

Standing Nude Arranging her Hair, 1930
Bronze
H. 157 cm

102

Woman and Crab, 1930
Bronze
16.5 x 15.5 x 12.5 cm

of possibilities. A Maillol statue is a perpetual revelation of the type of beauty which the sculptor invented. From 1921 to 1935, Maillol worked on his large public monuments (Céret, Port-Vendres, Elne, Banyuls, Basel). Concurrently he modelled statuettes which render a more intimate perception of the body. With small sculptures like *Woman and Crab* or *Woman with Thorn*, he extended the series of bathers and crouching women he had begun at the start of his career. The theme of the woman at her toilet first appeared in sculpture in the sixteenth century. The sculptor Ponce Jacquiot

is said to have pioneered it with a series of bronzes representing classical nymphs smoothing their hair, drying themselves, removing a thorn from a foot, and so forth. The suggested presence of water is merely a pretext for the sculptor to model a serene nude body.

To Maillol, the theme of the woman bathing was something of a paradox. Whether they are adolescent girls or mature women, his bathers, like Renoir's, unquestionably possess physical reality. Yet they are creations of the imagination and are never far removed from abstraction. Maillol had a predilection for rounded

Woman Holding her Foot, 1923
Terracotta
15 x 16 x 13.5 cm

La Méditerranée, 1923
Terracotta
18.2 x 13 x 10.4 cm

surfaces and curves, for they give compactness to the volumes of a sculpture. Two 1930 statuettes, *Thought* and *Crouching Woman*, are exemplary in this respect. Their pose refers only secondarily to reality. In each case, the sculpture is a small block of bronze articulating solid forms which verge on pure abstraction. These two works show us how far Maillol's art has evolved since his first Nabi statuettes. The beauty they express in almost abstract terms stems from plastic experiments based on a single idea – the idea of pushing simplification to an extreme. It was this quest for ever greater simplification that led Maillol to return again and again to the same subjects, the same themes; it was this which allowed him to spend ten years working on a sculpture. He shares this ideal of simplified outlines with his friend Matisse. Far from impoverishing his œuvre, it allowed him on the contrary to discover its hidden potentiality. Like Maillol, Matisse often turned back to earlier works in order to extend an idea they contain. His variations on female backs illustrate the parallels between the two artists' experiments. His *Backs I-IV* series is an object lesson in that it shows the artist laboring, stage by stage, to arrive at a composition from which everything inessential has been stripped away. Both artists have in common a conviction that simplified forms are based on an art of synthesis, and that it takes forty years to reduce a complex figure to a single line. As early as 1906, Maillol wrote to Maurice Denis apropos the Fauvist painters: They "all seem fine to me, but there's nothing like a canvas that has been caressed for a long time. The young are too easily satisfied. (…) It is certain that one ends up getting tired of even the most beautiful hasty sketch, whereas a work that's been carefully worked out satisfies one fully."

Maillol's quest for perfection can be seen in both his painting and his sculpture. To achieve the architectural mastery and the total simplification of contours he was pursuing, he was forever obliged to revise and refine the slope of his planes. This explains the large number of stages many of his works went through. Fifteen years of work went into *Venus with Necklace*.

Woman Crouching, 1930
Bronze
H. 16.5 cm

Thought, 1930
Bronze
H. 27.9 cm

Dina with Plait, 1940
Bronze
34 x 21 x 37 cm

"I waited fifteen years for the line of my Venus' legs. I added plaster... I removed it... I put it back. I had misgivings about it. All in vain! One fine day after fifteen years of this constantly renewed, constantly wasted labor punctuated by long periods of silence, after getting back (to Marly-le-Roi) from Banyuls, as I was standing in front of the statue which I had not set eyes on in six months, the line suddenly came to me... God knows, it looked simple enough. I've been working on this statue for fifteen years and all that's lacking now are the arms. They're clear in my mind. Now I only have to position them." He spun the statue slowly on its base, brushing it lightly with his fingertips. "This is the best part," he said, caressing the lines of the figure's right flank. "It is very difficult to do a standing woman."[2] He began by sculpting the torso without a head and without arms, then made a cast of it, which he reworked in plaster.

This torso, which dates from the year 1918, is a work of art in itself. It is perhaps one of the most accomplished pieces of sculpture in his entire œuvre. As Waldemar Georges puts it, Maillol's torsos "are not amputated, decapitated busts. They are organisms and are perhaps more complete than anatomies which imitate nature with its flaws, failings, and imperfections."[3] While visiting the Louvre with Count Kessler one day, Maillol stopped in front of a

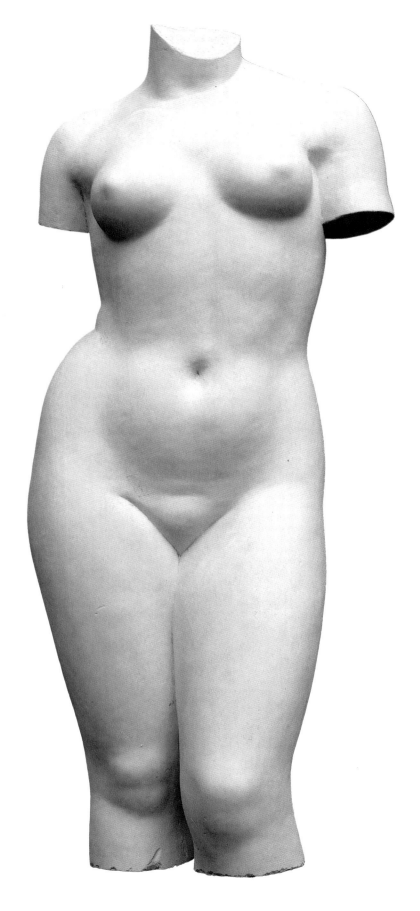

Torso of the Birth of Venus, 1918
Plaster
H. 120 cm

Following pages: Armless Venus, 1922 – Bronze – H. 176 cm / Venus, 1918-1928 – Bronze – H. 176 cm

statue of Venus which had lain in the sea off the coast of Africa for so long that its details had been rounded and simplified by the action of waves. Turning to his patron, the sculptor explained, "This figure shows me what is the essential plastic quality of a work of art. A sculpture must be beautiful even after the original surface has been lost and it has been worn down like a sea shell. This means that the essence of beauty endures all the same when one is in the presence of a true sculpture which possesses this miracle of harmony between its masses."[4]

Maillol subsequently executed two versions of *Venus*, with and without necklace. He also did a number of preparatory works, which include a woman holding a shawl with both hands raised. The plaster version, which he completed in 1928, was displayed at the Salon d'Automne and received considerable critical acclaim. It was later acquired by the London museum of modern art and is now to be seen in the Tate Gallery. Another casting of it, a gift of the sculptor's son Lucien, stands in the middle of the Place des Loges in Perpignan.

With the advent of the 1930s, Maillol undertook a new project, conceiving a group which he intended as a hymn to youth. Variously called *Nymphs in a Meadow* and *Three Graces* (a title which Maillol, who felt that its nudes were too "powerful" to be called this,

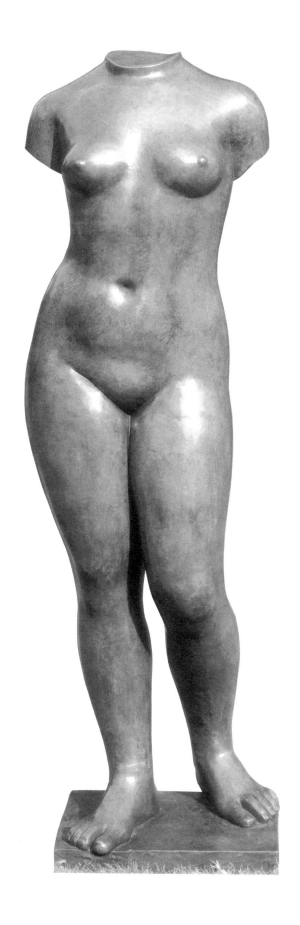

Nude Bather, detail, 1921
Bronze

Torso of Nymph, 1931
Bronze
H. 158 cm

111

disliked), the group consists of three figures and recalls Raphael's *Three Graces*. Each one of the three is based on an actual model. It took the sculptor five years to model the group, which was first shown in 1937 at the Petit Palais in Paris. Jean Girou's description of a work session in Maillol's studio at the time the sculptor was beginning one of the three figures, is worth quoting at some length. "Maillol is beginning afresh," writes Girou. "It is slow, continuous, invisible work, and Maillol is the only one to follow it in detail. The projected sculpture progresses step by step; with a terrible patience, he builds it up gradually, guiding it through multiple stages, touch after touch, improvement after improvement. But clay has a short life span; it has to be fired, or else imprisoned in plaster. The statue is born and, in its proportions, announces the monumental work it will eventually become. Once the plaster has been poured, Maillol is able to examine the work critically and decide how to pursue his goal of perfection. The problem is to overcome the following paradox: to create from the outside a form that must take on inner life; solely through lighting, to give motion to the motionlessness of planes, shadows, roundnesses, hollows, profiles, angles, perspectives. Maillol works and reworks the plaster, filing it down, scraping again, detail after detail. When an arm does not correspond to his conception, when a leg isn't turned the way he wants it to, he amputates it, dismembers it without hesitation. His studio is a veritable accident ward: legs, arms, head, torsos lie scattered about;

plasters cut into section by the hacksaw of a consciousness, a knowledge, and an art that reject facility. Maillol alone knows where his creation is going; his sculpture is a miracle of patience."[5]

Maillol began by sculpting the group's central figure, drawing his inspiraion for it from a model named Lucile; he asked his maid, Marie, to pose for the two other figures. As usual, he modelled several variations or "states" of each figure and produced torsos of each. The definitive sculpture has two versions, one with a base, the other without. Maillol always began modelling the torso, and only once he was satisfied with it did he add limbs. Adding limbs was always his greatest worry, especially when sculpting standing figures which provide few opportunities for a parallel arrangement of the arms or for folding them back on the torso. Reclining forms lend themselves better to parallel treatments, and seated figures naturally suggest limbs that fold on themselves. Maillol thought all the more highly of the *Venus of Milo* because it has come down to us armless: arms "would add nothing to its beauty," he declared; "on the contrary they would probably detract from it."[6]

Connecting limbs to the rest of the composition is one of the most difficult problems in sculpture. Maillol would alter the position of arms and legs from one version to the next in

Marie, detail, 1931
Bronze
H. 158 cm

order to compare their effect. In 1937, he went back to the figure of *Pomona* and changed the angle of her arms. The resulting version, the final *Pomona with Arms Lowered*, was exhibited at the Petit Palais in 1937 and was hailed as the crowning achievement of his art. His work was displayed in several rooms, and the critics unanimously acknowledged his genius. Yet, even at the height of fame, Maillol still received no public commissions. With the exception of his monuments to the war dead, his commissions all came from private quarters, usually committees organized by friends. Unperturbed by this state of affairs, the artist gratefully accepted honors and distinctions which he had never sought. Art was the only thing that mattered to him. In the last decade of his life it was to have an astonishing development.

Notes

[1] Jean Cassou, catalogue for the Maillol exhibition at the Museum of Modern Art, Paris, 1961.

[2] René Puig, "La vie misérable et glorieuse d'Aristide Maillol," *Tramontane* 49, 1965.

[3] Waldemar George, "Le sentiment antique dans l'art français," *L'amour de l'art*, 1935.

[4] Harry Kessler, preface to the Maillol exhibition at the Goupil Gallery, Londres, October 1928.

[5] Jean Girou, *Sculpteurs du Midi*, Floury, Paris, 1938.

[6] Pierre Camo, *Maillol mon ami*, Éd. du Grand-Chêne, Lausanne, 1950, p. 69.

The Nymph (armless), 1930
Bronze
H. 131 cm

The Three Nymphs, 1930 – Bronze – H. 157 cm

The Nymph, 1930
Bronze
H. 156 cm

Pomona with Arms Lowered,
1937
Bronze – H. 168 cm

CHAPTER VI

The painter, draftsman, and engraver

In France the art of sculpture was renewed by painters toward the end of the nineteenth century. Daumier, Degas, Renoir, and Gauguin have left us works which differ radically from *fin de siècle* academic art. With Matisse, Picasso, and Léger, Maillol was one of the handful of painters-cum-sculptors who transformed the art of statuary in the twentieth century. Maillol discovered his vocation as an artist through painting, and took up sculpture as an enjoyable sideline. Does this mean, as Michel Seuphor suggests, that for Maillol the two activities, painting and sculpture, were interrelated? "They complete each other, for nothing is ever complete, and the fact is, painters have brought something new to sculpture when they sought relaxation in it from the pressures of their own art. The painter and his independence have given *another* territory to sculpture, which seemed permanently frozen and incapable of understanding itself."[1] To Maillol, sculpture provided the answer he had been seeking in his experiments with synthesizing forms in

Dina with Scarf, 1941
Oil on canvas
110 x 95 cm

his early paintings. Even after becoming a sculptor, he never gave up painting altogether. All his life he remained close friends with painters: Bonnard, Louis Valtat, Matisse, Vuillard. Matisse's work on line and pure color interested him deeply, as did Bonnard's experiments with dissolving forms and light. "A painting should be a succession of spots which relate to each other and end by forming an object over which the eye travels smoothly," wrote the artist of the *Large Dark Nude.*

Gauguin's decisive influence in the years that followed Maillol's visit to the Café Volpini shifted the latter's painting toward treating figures against perspectiveless backgrounds. The future sculptor was fascinated with the art of frescos because, like tapestry-making, it eschews perspective. In the 1890s, he painted frescos in the villa of Count d'Esmont at Fécamp. One of the characteristics of his painting is the way he isolates a figure or face and anchors it to the picture plane.

The Nabis' concept of painting treated as an arrangement of flat planes on a canvas derives more from their discovery of Japanese art than from their interest in Cézanne's work. It is easy to see why Puvis de Chavannes played such an important role for them and why they admired the simplicity and monumentality of his frescos at the Pantheon.

In fact, Puvis marked young Maillol's painting well before the encounter with Gauguin. "If I had continued to paint, I would have let myself be influenced by Renoir. I did some paintings which resemble his. I could easily imitate him, whereas Courbet cannot be imitated. (…) Then I did some very insipid pictures. I got over this insipidness by doing still lifes. Having no one to turn to for advice, I tried to find my own guidance by studying the pictures of great artists; and that is how I turned to Puvis de Chavannes' example when I painted the portrait of my aunt at Banyuls."[2] Notice what Maillol says here about the role that still lifes played in his painting and about his interest in Puvis' frescos – an interest that was to revive in the thirties.

In the end, not only did Maillol develop a painting that was very different from Renoir's,

Back of Nude Bather, 1941
Red chalk and pastel
21 x 33 cm

but it was he who got the great painter interested in sculpture. Sculpture claimed so much of Maillol's time and energy that he no longer had any time to paint. One could say that he did the opposite of what a painter like Renoir practiced: he painted as a way of relaxing between doing sculpture.

Later he took up painting again by doing still lifes and taking a renewed interest in fresco-making. With his friend, the sculptor Pimienta, he travelled to Italy to study the painting of Raphael and Michelangelo, especially the Sistine Chapel frescos. This attraction to Michelangelo's painting can no doubt be explained by the fact that Maillol was returning to painting after years of sculpting the volumes of the human anatomy.

Maillol's return to painting did not happen all at once. Actually, he had never wholly stopped painting. He had continued the experiments he had begun in his Nabi years by painting nudes whenever he was able to get hold of a model. In 1930, he painted the *Pearly Nude* which clearly shows the new direction his painting was to take in the coming years. His palette was still limited to a few tones, but now he sought to intensify the brightness of his colors. He had a predilection for the theme of the nude seen from the back, and rendered it in numerous drawings and pastels; he was also drawn to the theme of large nudes in a

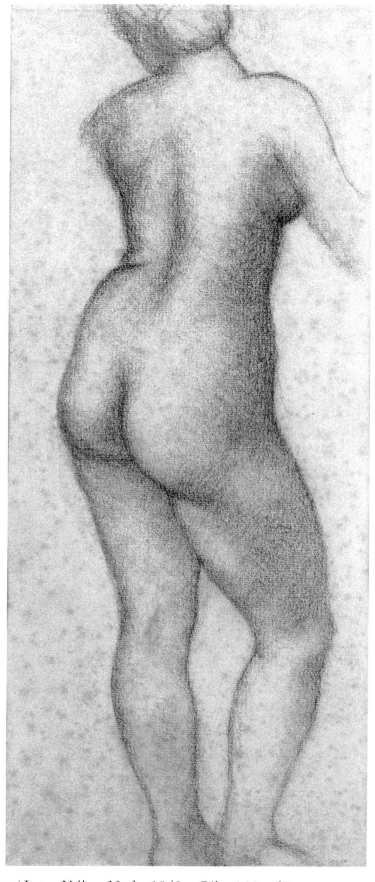

Back of Nude Bather, 1940
Red chalk
38 x 22 cm

Following pages: Seathed Bather, 1938 – Oil – 116 x 90 cm / Large Yellow Nude, 1943 – Oil – 100 x 62 cm

landscape, as well as to that of two nudes facing each other in a play on mirror images.

He discarded the flat treatment and surface effects of his Nabi-inspired pictures. It is easy to understand his interest in the art of Michelangelo, another sculptor-painter, and his preoccupation with rendering an impression of volumes by pictorial means. He evolved from a rather hieratic painting to a painting that seeks to translate three-dimensional forms into a two-dimensional language representing not only the sensuality of the nude but, as in his sculpture, the body's masses.

A few of the canvases he painted between 1937 and 1939, such as the *Blonde Bather*, show Maillol borrowing from the fresco technique to express a monumental body in painting. His work with Dina Vierny stimulated his desire to paint. He painted numerous pictures, including a *Homage to Gauguin* which shows a naked woman recalling the older painter's Tahitians, in a field of wheat – a sort of

The Two Friends, 1941
Oil on panel
21 x 33 cm

Portrait of Dina, 1940 – Oil on canvas – 55 x 47 cm

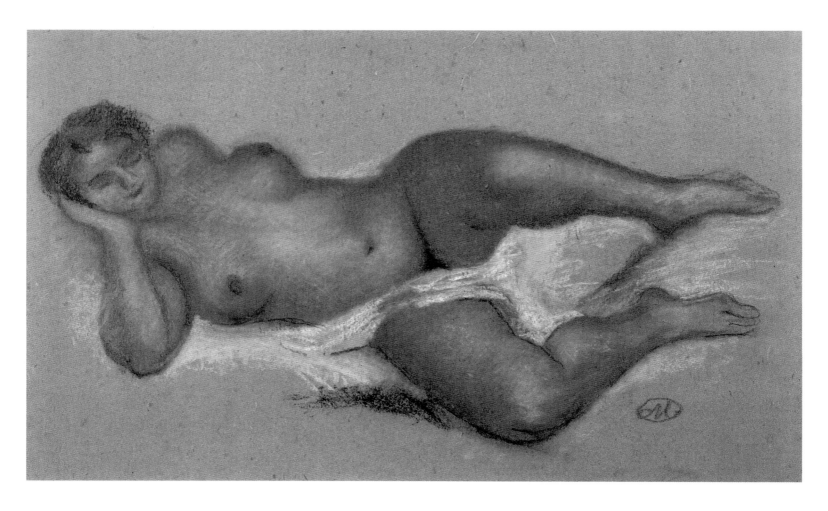

Recumbent Dina with Drapery
Charcoal, pastel, and chalk
21.5 x 35 cm

Mediterranean equivalent of the latter's Pacific idols. Maillol also invented new postures, different from those he rendered in his sculpture, to try and enhance his work on the beauty of the nude body. Sculpture had allowed him to invent a canon of beauty, a synthesis of forms that drew inspiration from, but owed nothing to, reality. Painting forced him to return to the tactile, material representation of the subject. He felt capable of doing a sculptor's painting, where the architecture of the nude, which had been pure volumes in sculpture, becomes image, colors, sensuality.

He wanted to express substance and make the sense of touch perceptible to the eye. In their essence, his *Bathers* are as abstract as are the figures he sculpted: they are the architecture of a type of beauty. But they also constitute a pure presence, an actual substance within a picture whose renderings of flesh, whose curves, refer to a vision of the material world. A painting like *Dina with Scarf* has nothing to do with the frigid, eternal beauty of Platonic myths, but belongs to a world of harmony that is both alive and timeless. Just as Cézanne in his still lifes strives to express the structure of an apple rather than its content, Maillol does not represent a graceful bather, but the enduring form of that which changes. Maillol's painting in the final years of his life is a painting beyond representation, a painting born from image as his sculpture is born from significance. He painted a variety of subjects – nudes, portraits of Dina, landscapes such as the 1943 Provençal *Mas Among Vineyards,* and still lifes like the *Sunflowers* of 1940 or the 1943 *Pomegranates*.

To an even greater extent than either painting or sculpture, drawing remained Maillol's busiest activity; it was a kind of daily writing for him; he relied on it to develop ideas for his œuvre. "This is how I work," he once explained to Alfred Kühn, showing him an ordinary note book on each page of which he had sketched ideas for a female statuette: the same figure standing, walking, crouching, often nude, but also clothed in such a way that the interplay of muscles and movement were always visible. "I do all of this in the street – it's all drawn from nature. You say that girls don't walk around naked. True enough! But I undress them. I fill one notebook every month."[3]

But drawing was not just a script which allowed Maillol to note down forms that caught his eye; it already constituted style and was an accurate translation of his thought. Maillol wanted to express volumes rather than

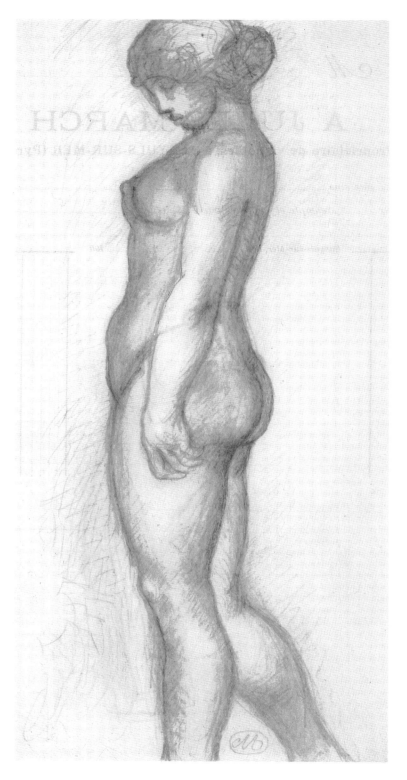

Profile of Young Girl, 1899
Pencil
27 x 21.5 cm

outlines. Unlike Rodin, who saw drawing in terms of the arabesque, a quick notation of modelling in fine looping lines; and unlike Degas, who tracked down his subject like a mathematician, by successive approximations, Maillol was not obsessed with truth to life. He wanted his art to be alive rather than scrupulously accurate. "Everything becomes soft and round, the contours as well as the internal drawing. They are inseparable as a matter of fact, since the first are merely the second extending to the surface. The artist likes to use a soft pencil or red chalk which leaves a rich trace. The line acquires values of light and shadow; it completes the masses which are indicated by supple, irregular hatchings that caress the body's curves, and occasionally, if the colored background lends itself to this, by chalk highlights."[4]

With his large pastels and admirable red chalk drawings, Maillol belongs to the tradition of great eighteenth-century draftsmen such as Boucher and Fragonard. His pastels show the same loving, velvety treatment of flesh expressing a charmed contemplation of a body in a lascivious pose and the first

Nude Lying Against Green Background, 1935
Pastel, pencil, and chalk
22 x 35 cm

The Art of Love, 1935
Red chalk
34 x 25.5 cm

stirrings of erotic feeling. Each of his drawings is a formal translation of desire and admiration for the warm curves of a beautiful nude. His drawing is at once an object of experimentation and an inquiry into forms. Though his sculpture invokes serenity, it nevertheless draws on poses which bring the curves of the body into play and emphasize its roundnesses. Maillol was especially interested in the pelvis and upper thighs and in the strong thrust of the torso. He worked on his drawing more for his own purposes than for the pleasure of art-lovers, and left many of his studies unfinished. He made no effort to define facial expressions and features, and showed little interest in arms. He attached more importance to representing feet, whose elementary shapes, he felt, were more in harmony with the rest of the body, than hands, traditionally a favorite subject with draftsmen.

John Rewald observes that Maillol made two rather different types of drawing. There are the drawings based on an actual model and which, independently of the degree to which he pushes their execution, clearly show a concern not to stray from the facts of the human body. And then there are the drawings from memory, which are almost always inspired by some decorative preocccupation: their simplified lines harmonize and generalize forms in order to obtain compositions in which the body is, so to speak, nothing more than a pretext for linear interactions of a stunning beauty.[5]

In the drawings of Maillol's final period, he was able to combine decorative experiments with a faithful rendering of the model – as in his paintings which fuse observation and an imaginative recreation of nature – but he never yielded to a love of line for its own sake; under his hands, line was always subordinate to form. As John Rewald has remarked very perspicaciously, even in his decorative drawings the lines are never totally imaginary, but are always suggested by observed forms. All of his sketches (some of which he worked on at length) spring from direct observation, even though they were often completed from memory. Maillol would sometimes keep a drawing in a portfolio for years and would then suddenly remember it and use it as an idea for a sculpture. He found his drawings gave him valuable insights in how to connect an arm to a shoulder, how to render the bend of a hip, what angle to give a torso. Donatello once said, "I can teach you the art of making statues with a single word: drawing!" By pursuing the one line in a thousand that is absolutely right, Maillol built up his statues and infused them with a profound sense of revealed beauty.

He would use the line he developed in his drawing, especially the decorative line, to illustrate books and develop a large body of engravings alongside his sculptural œuvre. In this respect, he can be said to belong to the company of artists who also engraved: Matisse, Picasso, Bonnard, Rouault. He undertook to do

Back View of Dina Arranging her Hair, 1944
Pastel, charcoal, and chalk
37 x 25 cm

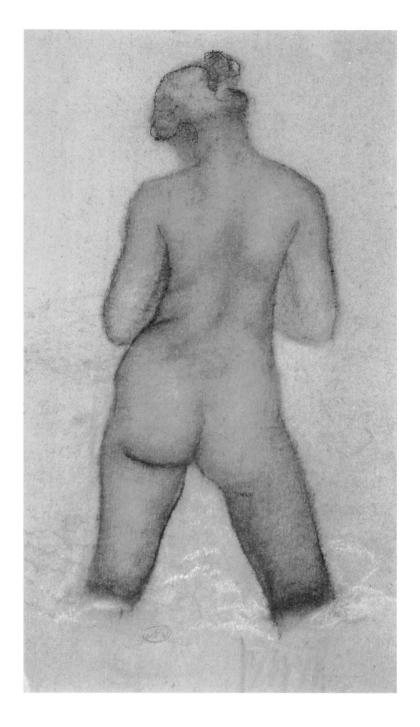

Dina from the Back, 1944
Pastel
38 x 22 cm

his first engravings on Gauguin's advice, in the late 1890s. Among the works of this early period that have come down to us are woodcuts like a *Hero and Leander* which belonged to Daniel de Monfreid and an *Eve and the Serpent*, which reminds us of Gauguin and the influence he had on Maillol in the last years of the nineteenth century.

Although Maillol was sometimes critical of the illustrative aspect of much engraving, he was a great admirer of the graphic work of such masters as Odilon Redon, whose "black" prints are suffused with a mysterious atmosphere which fascinated Maillol. "I detest illustrated books," he once said. "I do them because I do not consider line engraving on wood to be illustration; drawings done in this way are the equivalent of typographical characters. I believe that they're typography." Count Kessler, who conceived the project of having Marc Lafargue translate the *Eclogues* of Virgil and publishing it in a limited edition, held similar views. He owned the Cranach Press in Weimar, a fine press run by William Morris' master, Emery Walker.

When Kessler asked Maillol to do the illustrations, the sculptor agreed. Both patron and artist wanted to produce books in which illustrations and typography would be closely interrelated instead of being placed side by side without much connection, as in most modern illustrated books.[6] In order to link the book's typography to its drawings, Kessler wanted to revive the fonts used by the eighteenth-century master Nicolas Jenson. Kessler saw in the

The Wave, 1888
Woodcut
17.1 x 19.7 cm

Two Women in the Grass
Lithograph
20 x 25 cm

(DIE ECLOGEN VERGILS

IN DER URSPRACHE UND DEUTSCH ÜBERSETZT VON RUDOLF ALEXANDER SCHROEDER : MIT ILLUSTRATIONEN

GEZEICHNET UND GESCHNITTEN VON ARISTIDE MAILLOL

The Eclogues of Virgil, 1926
Woodcut

classical, full forms of Jenson's "monumental and simple" typeface a possible source of inspiration for the illustrations. There was after all a precedent for this approach in the volumes of the fifteenth-century Italian printers who provided the artists of the Quattrocento with the basis for an illustrative technique derived from the spirit of the printed characters. "We agreed," writes Kessler, "on a typeface designed by the great Venetian printer Jenson. Not an antique typeface, it was monumental, possessed inner tension and a soft luminousness."[7]

Between 1910 and 1913, Maillol executed forty-three woodcut illustrations and worked on some twenty-five other woodcuts of initial letters. His love of good-quality materials and his taste for perfection led him to invent and hand-manufacture "Montval" paper with the help of his nephew Gaspard Maillol. The *Eclogues* were published in 1926. To illustrate Virgil's idylls he gave free rein to his imagination. Rendering leaves, for example, he revived the sinuous decorative line of his Nabi period. He filled the book with drawings of simplified Arcadian scenes which have a rich fragrance of the antique. Indeed his illustrations and the text combine to create an impression of pervasive harmony. His drawing is simplified to the extreme and his style of engraving "as sharp as a primitive's." A knife, a hollow chisel, and a small metal rule were his only tools.

Maillol made not only woodcuts but lithographs as well, notably for a volume of poems, *Belle Chair*, by Emile Verhaeren. But undoubtedly one of his most beautiful art books is the edition of Ovid's *Art of Love* published by the Lausanne printer Gonin in 1935. Here Maillol translated the verses of the Latin poet into glowing plastic lines, celebrating physical love in a series of Dionysiac scenes. Gonin also published an edition of Longus' *Daphnis and Chloe*, as well as a volume of Virgil's *Georgics*

Daphnis and Chloe, 1937
Preparatory drawing and woodcut
9.9 x 11.9 cm

(which appeared only after Maillol's death). Another art publisher, Ambroise Vollard, commissioned Maillol to illustrate an edition of Ronsard's *Livre des Folastries*, for which the sculptor executed forty-three etchings. Maillol's graphic œuvre, which spans a large variety of techniques of engraving and book illustration, is exceptionally rich; with its diversity and beauty, it has all the hallmarks of his genius.

Notes

[1] Michel Seuphor, *La Sculpture de ce siècle*, Éd. du Griffon, Neuchâtel, 1959.

[2] Judith Cladel, *Maillol*, Grasset, Paris, 1937, p. 39.

[3] Alfred Kühn, *Maillol*, Seemann, Leipzig, 1925.

[4] Pierre du Colombier, *Maillol, Dessins et Pastels*, Galerie Louis Carré, December 1941.

[5] John Rewald, "Souvenirs de Maillol," in the catalogue for the Maillol exhibition in Japan, 1984, p. 43.

[6] Judith Cladel, *op. cit.*, p. 106.

[7] Harry Kessler, "Pourquoi Maillol a illustré Les Eglogues de Virgile," *Der Querschnitt* VIII, November 1928, pp. 768-772.

Chapter VII

The final years

The exhibition mounted in 1937 at the Petit Palais in Paris was the greatest tribute to Maillol in the artist's lifetime; it also gave a measure of the influence of his sculpture on his contemporaries. Maillol pioneered a unique, highly personal approach to the art of statuary and it set him apart from the other great sculptors of his age such as Despiau, Bourdelle, and Laurens. His investigation of the architecture of the body and of volumes in general inspired a whole generation of sculptors: Jeanne Poupelet, Henri Parayre, Marcel Gimond Schnegg, Wlérick Manolo, and many others. One cannot avoid being struck by the homogeneity of their output: it is as if all these artists shared a common heritage.

As Jacques Lassaigne wrote in 1937, "To them, Maillol is a great deal more than a teacher, he is a fact of life... The role of great creators is above all to free their followers from error and ignorance. It was not in books and museums that Maillol found the eternal human language, but within himself. The myth of Maillol the pious heir of the Greeks has been exploded: he is young and fresh, and if he comes close to them, it is unwittingly. Everything he has created constitutes a heritage of certainties that is liberating our young sculpture from exhausting researches and smoothly ushering it in to the province of clarity."[1]

Indeed the clarity of Maillol's forms, the coherence of the figures born from his architectonic concept of sculpture, were an inspiration for artists like André Deluol, Littman, Raymond Martin, Yencesse and Robert Couturier (who was to become one of Maillol's rougher-outs and was to collaborate on the monumental statue, *The River*). The artist of *La Méditerranée* did not teach; he gave advice, sometimes guided young sculptors who came to him, but was never a teacher in the strict sense, for his art was not based on any theory. Nevertheless Maillol's concept of forms commanded great respect, and his influence during the years before World War II was enormous. At a time when a strong current of realist figuration was emerging in sculpture, Maillol seemed light-years ahead of contemporary theory. His work, though it did not hark back to the past, was viewed as a model by the artists of the thirties

The Mountain, detail, 1937
Lead
Paris, Tuileries Gardens

who were endeavoring to revive figuration. By now in his seventies, Maillol was working on several projects at once, and his inspiration flowed as rich as ever.

He had always been looking for a model who would allow him to crystallize his ideas, and confided this preoccuption to his friend Dondelle, the architect of the Museum of Modern Art at the Palais de Tokyo in Paris. Dondelle told him about a young woman of Russian origin who bore a remarkable physical resemblence to some of the artist's sculptures. Encouraged by this, Maillol promptly wrote to her as follows: "Mademoiselle, I am told that you look like a Maillol or a Renoir. I'd settle for a Renoir." This is how he and Dina Vierny met. They were to work together for the next decade. The appearance of this new model in Maillol's life brought about a renewal of his art and gave him the impetus to create the monumental sculptures of his final years. "I began posing for large monumental drawings and for the carving of the *Nymphs*," remembers Dina Vierny. "Next came *The Mountain*, for which he

The Mountain, detail, 1937
Lead
165 x 185 cm

returned to projects he had had at the beginning of his life, but with a certain change in the conceptions that determined his work. He wanted to complete the monuments he carried within himself and then come back to painting, which is in fact what he did."[2] *The Mountain* was commissioned by the Museum of Modern Art in Paris. Maillol started out with the pose of a seated woman which he had imagined as early as the year 1900. It was a figure to which he often returned in his career, tirelessly seeking to reconstruct the articulation of its volumes. He sculpted several statuettes as preliminary studies before moving on to the monumental figure.

The Mountain concluded the cycle of seated women which had begun with *La Méditerranée* and had included *Night*, the Céret monument and *Grief*. By working on a monumental scale, Maillol hoped to attain stability, immobility, and massiveness. Henri Focillon writes apropos monumental sculpture that it involves two different types of space: space as a limit and space as an environment. "In rendering a limit, the sculptor assumes there are two spaces: the space in which we move about (...) and the space of the object. That is to say, not only its position in our space, but also its own inner space."[3] Monumental sculpture, and outdoor sculpture in particular, must emphasize space as a limit and occupy it with its mass. "This art tends toward the block, toward density, toward fewer shadows, the peace of light, the wall's unity. (...) Space conceived as a limit is the space of the archaic Greeks, of Romanesque art, and of some contemporary sculptors."[4] In contrast, space as an environment is more likely to produce a scattering of matter, eloquence, and movement. Monumentality allowed Maillol to bring out a quality that is inherent in all his sculpture: its ability to measure itself against open space. His monumental sculptures can be counted among the truly successful *plein air* statues: they succeed wholly in subordinating surface to interiority. John Rewald states that what Maillol wanted was to bring sculpture back to the earth, to make it aware of its own weight and of a certain classical stability. This mattered far more to him than the fascinating fusion of form and light, movement and illusion, that produced so many of Rodin's masterpieces.[5]

In 1937, Maillol completed the stone version of *The Mountain* which now belongs to the Museum of Modern Art in Paris. The years 1937-1938 inaugurated the period of large monumental works like *Air* and *The River*. Maillol was commissioned by the City of Toulouse to sculpt a monument to the pilots of France's pioneering airmail service, l'Aéropostale, who had been killed in the line of duty. A meeting was arranged at Marly-le-Roi between the sculptor and the famous pilot Jean Mermoz. Maillol agreed to undertake the project and moved to the Hotel Miramar, which was located next to a large warehouse where he

Air, 1938
Lead
139 x 255 cm

could carve the statue in stone. First, however, he modelled the figure in plaster.

John Rewald visited Maillol's studio as the latter was working on the monument: "As I was taking leave of him, the artist told me to follow him and conducted me to the warehouse behind the studio to show me a new sculpture. It was the Toulouse monument, *Air*. Against the dark background of planks and leaves where one could make out the *Monument to Cézanne* in the shadows, shone the magnificent, lissome nude of a huge young girl with outstretched limbs. (…) The artist explained that he had proceded as he usually does when making his small statuettes, often removing their arms, legs, and head in order to give them different poses and thus create a new work. Maillol had a large plaster of the *Monument to*

Cézanne cut into sections, which he used to assemble the figure for *Air*. (...) By this means, modifying the pose of the body, adjusting the members differently, the artist was able to create or obtain a work which is not only totally different, but seems, if possible, even more beautiful than the initial statue. Thus, thanks to a small maquette which dates from approximately thirty years earlier, and thanks to the elements drawn from the *Monument to Cézanne*, a new work was born."[6]

Resting on an imaginary center of gravity, *Air* seems to float in space. The volume of this slender body teeters on the border between immobility and movement. Light is diffused subtly over it, accentuating the planes, emphasizing the modelling, softening the contours; shadows and highlights are delicately opposed to each other, and, instead of isolating the different parts of the statue, the lighting gives the work density. "I want light," Maillol declared; "what I am looking for is the volume in air. The statue in atmosphere, in light and air. Clearly I'm obliged to search for the larger form. I'm not interested in modelling a finger accurately from nature."[7]

All of Maillol's thought seems to be expressed in those words. From the first, this artist wanted to infuse the forms he invented with life, but without falling into the realist tradition. Each one of his sculptures transmutes inert matter into a living form. He does not mold the forms of nature in order to assemble them in a sculpture; rather he invents proportions which transform the representation of the human body into a statue governed by the laws of perspective and architecture. He admired the great statues in the gardens at Versailles; they were one of his sources of inspiration, no doubt because the eighteenth-century artists knew how to combine sculpture and achitecture. The Versailles statues are not mere elements of decoration; they are part of the architectural structure of the palace gardens and buildings. But Maillol's real fascination with the outdoor sculptures of Coysevox and Coustou had also to do with the kind of lead that gives them their soft, bluish patina. He decided to re-use this medium which had long fallen into abeyance in sculpture. All of his large monumental sculptures are cast in lead: the *Monument to Cézanne*, *Air*, and *The River*, which he began around 1938.

Yet again it was the sculptor's old friend Frantz Jourdain who organized a committee and raised funds for a monument to honor a great man – this time, Henri Barbusse. The statue, which Maillol was commissioned to sculpt, has sometimes been called *The Sorrows of War* – an appropriate title for a tribute to the author of *Le Feu* and other books which denounce man's destructive insanity – but we now know it as *The River*. Maillol employed the young sculptor Robert Couturier as rougherout, and immediately set to work on the monument. He re-used the figure of *The Mountain*,

Air, detail, 1938
Plaster
Studio photograph

Following pages: The River, 1938-1943 – Lead – 124 x 230 x 163 cm

which he cut into segments that he recombined into a totally different pose. "One Sunday morning," recalls Couturier, "we had moved the different parts of *The Mountain*. Maillol then left. When he returned we got back to work, and out of this came *The River*. He instructed me what to do, and on the plaster one can see his emendations and additions to *The Mountain*. He said, 'I want to do something dramatic, but not too dramatic, something dignified like Racine.' The base of the first version didn't satisfy him, and he wondered if the statue shouldn't rest directly on the ground."8 The sculptor did three versions of *The River*, two of them with base, the third without.

The problem of whether to give a statue a base or not, and, if so, what type of base, put the very concept of the monument, as Maillol understood it, into question. A monument, he felt, should not be a demonstration of virtuosity placed above the viewer, but should on the contrary be primarily a work of art. Bringing down the monument from its heights was part of his aesthetic program. Monumentality does not require to be looked up to, but simply to be looked at. This was a radically new concept of the function of monumental sculpture, for it introduced a new relationship between the statue and the viewer. It brought down the sculpture to eye level. *The River* is one of the most tension-filled and tormented of Maillol's works. The figure appears to be swept by a momentum that no human power can contain. The head expresses a kind of terror and the hands seem to be trying to arrest the current that is sweeping it along. A premonition?

The outbreak of World War II interrupted Maillol's work. The German offensive against France in May 1940 caught him by surprise in Banyuls. He stayed on in the unoccupied zone, isolated and far from his studio at Marly. A few visitors called on him and brought fresh news of the war: Robert Couturier, his old friend Pierre Camo, John Rewald on his way to the United States, and his model Dina Vierny, with whom he continued to work. For, despite everything, he never stopped working, unlike his experience during World War I. Never particularly inclined to meditativeness, he became increasingly contemplative. He set little store in his own life, yet continued to look at life as a source of inspiration for his art.

Though he refused to have anything to do with the occupiers, he was unable to prevent German officers who admired his work from coming to see him. Picasso received the same kind of attention in his atelier on Rue des Grands-Augustins in Paris. In 1942, an exhibition of works by Arno Brekker, the official sculptor of the Third Reich, was organized at the Orangerie in Paris. Maillol was invited to the opening and made the mistake of accepting, mainly because it gave him an opportunity to cross over into the occupied zone and visit his studio at Marly-le-Roi to check on the state of the sculptures he had been obliged to

Dina, without base, 1937
Bronze
H. 20.3 cm

abandon there. He was totally unaware of the political significance of this act, which was bitterly held against him. Later, he was wrongly accused of having collaborated with the Germans, and his detractors recalled that he had had links with Germany before the war (though in fact they went back to before World War I). It was even said that he had travelled to Berlin in 1941 with a number of other French painters and sculptors, which was of course false. Lieutenant Heller, the German officer who accompanied him to the Brekker show, recalls in his memoirs that Maillol showed no enthusiasm whatsoever for Brekker's work but rejoiced on meeting several of his artist friends he had not seen since the outbreak of the war. Heller also states that the sculptor never for a moment imagined that his presence at the Orangerie could have any serious repercussions.

The truth is that Maillol spent the war years in Banyuls, devoting himself totally to his researches and working with his model. When the latter informed him of her activities in the Resistance and her efforts to help people wanted by the Germans to flee France, he immediately offered to let her use his studio in the village of Puig del Las as a refuge. He also showed her a safe passage over the Pyrenees, and in fact the first clandestine network to spirit people across the border into Spain was called "*le réseau* Maillol."

A veritable mountain hermit, Maillol spent the war years working on his last sculpture. *Harmony* is in fact his testament, a summing up of forty years of sculpting. "I want this work to be more realist and alive than anything I have done up until now. That is why I am for once working directly from a model, and not just from drawings, as I usually do. However, my drawings are a great help to me and I continue to do lots of them. Right now I'm making hundreds of sketches from every imaginable angle, so that she will become what I want her to be."[9] As usual, Maillol modelled several versions, endlessly re-working each one of his studies, adding an extra layer of thickness in one place, then removing it, polishing and repolishing, indefatigable in his quest for perfection, doggedly pursuing the "idea" that he had wanted to realize from the very first. Observing the sculptor at work in front of his posing model, Rewald noted, "It was obvious that the model was only a guide for the sculptor, and how obstinently he pursued his initial idea (…) one could almost say in spite of the harmonious forms which this beautiful creature was offering!"[10]

Harmony: how is one to understand this "idea" which runs through Maillol's entire œuvre, this abstract concept of the beautiful, as opposed to its physical reality? Maillol explains it as follows: "For Plato, idea and form were identical, and that is how I too understand it. It is a form and a preconceived idea that guides the artist. Followed by gracefulness, power, and all the other qualities which accrue in the

Sketch for Harmony, detail, 1940
Bronze
H. 154 cm

course of the work, and as a result the work is not just the realization of an idea, of an intellectual conception, but is also a work of art."[11] *Harmony* was never completed; it sums up the thought of an artist who, at the end of his life, was still asking his friends Bonnard and Matisse, "Have I made any progress?" It was on his way to visit another friend, Raoul Dufy, that Maillol was grievously injured in a car crash. He died on September 27, 1944. In the chaos of the times, his death went well nigh unnoticed.

Later, Maillol's son Lucien and Dina Vierny organized a state funeral for the sculptor at Banyuls. Then, with the help of the Minister of Culture, André Malraux, Dina Vierny created an open air Maillol museum in the Tuileries Gardens in Paris, where she had eighteen of his major works installed. It had been one of the artist's deepest wishes to have a sculpture garden. "Give me a garden," he had once said, "and I will fill it with statues." For the first time, *La Méditerranée*, *Night*, *Action in Chains*, *The Nymphs*, *The Seasons*, the *Monument to Cézanne*, the *Monument to the Dead of Port-Vendres*, *Air*, and *The River* were put on display together.

Finally, in 1994, Dina Vierny established the Maillol Museum in the Hôtel Bouchardon on Rue de Grenelle in Paris. The museum's mission is to reveal the importance of the role that Maillol's œuvre played in modern art. How was the sculptor's thought able to bring forth such a varied œuvre from the pursuit of a single idea? Maillol's concept of form, worked and reworked endlessly until it attained the absolute interiority of pure sculpture, has left a deep imprint on the history of statuary. The influence of his heritage can be felt among numerous artists who admired the architecture of his smooth, polished forms: Arp, Brancusi, Laurens, and so many others – including Moore who once confessed that as a young man he had wanted to call on Maillol, whom he revered, but had been too shy to knock at his door. Maillol himself is said to have been too shy to speak to Gauguin the first time he met that artist. Thus history repeats itself...

Yet though his art dominated the age and inspired countless artists, Maillol himself remained indifferent to fame and honors, and in his old age came increasingly to resemble a Greek sage. "I'm enjoying myself," he declared; "nothing is eternal. People have a mania for thinking they're heros! Everything that I have done – tapestry, ceramics, engraving – I've done because it amused me. For me, art doesn't have the seriousness, the terrible importance it has for the members of the Institut de France. One doesn't kill oneself for botching a work; one makes another one."[12]

Notes

[1] Jacques Lassaigne, *Almanach des Arts*, 1937.
[2] Dina Vierny in conversation with the author.
[3] Henri Focillon, *L'art des sculpteurs romans*, Paris, 1931, p. 27.
[4] *Ibid.*, pp. 27-28.
[5] John Rewald, "Souvenirs de Maillol," in the catalogue of the 1984 Maillol exhibition in Japan, p. 40.
[6] *Ibid.*, p. 43.
[7] Alfred Kühn, *op. cit.*, p. 4.
[8] Robert Couturier in conversation with the author 1991.
[9] John Rewald, *op. cit.*, pp. 44-45.
[10] John Rewald, *op. cit.*, p. 45.
[11] John Rewald, *op. cit.*, p. 37.
[12] Judith Cladel, *Maillol*, Paris, Grasset, 1937, p. 134.

Harmony, 1940-1944 – Bronze – H. 162 cm

Aristide Maillol at Marly-le-Roi in 1937. Photo Brassaï

The country near Banyuls, with the Maillol family farm. Now the Maillol Museum

Chronology

1852

Marriage of Raphaël Maillol, a shop assistant at Banyuls-sur-Mer, and Catherine Rougé, a salesgirl. They were to have five children: Raphaël, Adolphe, Marie, Aristide, and Elisa.

1861

Birth of Aristide Bonaventure Jean Maillol on December 8. His birthplace, Banyuls-sur-Mer, is a small port on the Mediterranean coast, dominated by the Albères mountains whose slopes are covered with vineyards and olive groves. Because of the neighboring Spanish border, smuggling is a favorite local occupation. Young Aristide is enthralled by the stories of his grandfather, a fisherman and sometime smuggler. He is raised by his aunt Lucie. His childhood is sad and lonely. He attends the village school, where he meets Edouard Villarem, who will remain a lifelong friend.

1871

Death of Maillol's brother, Adolphe Simon, a woodcarver who specialized in animals. The first blow in the future sculptor's life.

Hills in the vicinity of Banyuls

1874

Maillol completes his primary schooling and is enrolled by his aunt in a boarding school, the Collège Saint-Louis, in nearby Perpignan. He will always remember his days there with boredom. To relieve his loneliness, his aunt Lucie comes to visit him regularly once a week. He paints his first painting, a view of the port of Banyuls (*La Passe d'Ouve*), at the age of thirteen.

1877

Death of his father. This reduces the family's income to the produce from its vineyards.

1879

Expelled from his school in Perpignan and returns to Banyuls, where he decides to become a painter. He publishes the one and only copy of *La Figue* (later re-named *Le Journal d'un Ennuyé*). He is the magazine's sole editor, printer, illustrator, and reader.

1880

The family vineyards destroyed by the phylloxera pest. The Maillols lose their only source of income.

1881

Returns to Perpignan to take drawing lessons at the Musée Hyacinthe Rigaud under his former teacher at the Collège Saint-Louis, Hyacinthe Alchimovitch. Having rapidly absorbed all that the latter and the museum's collections were able to offer him, he decides to pursue his art studies in Paris. His aunt Lucie, on whom he is financially dependent, strongly disapproves, but in the end reluctantly agrees to his plan. Overcoming her provincial prejudice against artists and their bohemian ways, she offers to send him a monthly allowance of twenty francs. Contenting himself with this pittance, Maillol leaves for Paris, where he rents a room on Rue des Vertus and takes his meals at the home of his former primary school teacher, at number 10 Rue des Gravilliers. He is lonely and homesick, but refuses to be discouraged. Like many young artists struggling to survive in *fin de siècle* Paris, he is penniless. He makes several attempts to pass the entrance examination at the École des Beaux-Arts and fails.

1882

Enrolls as an auditor in the antique drawing classes at the Beaux-Arts, under the painter and sculptor Gérome, who is one of the chief upholders of official art and academicism. Hoping to show his work to Gérome, Maillol calls on him at his studio on Boulevard de Clichy. Gérome receives him stretched out on the floor, painting a canvas. He glances at Maillol's studies and tells him, "You know nothing! Go to the École des Arts Décoratifs and work on noses and ears." Undiscouraged, Maillol continues to frequent the Beaux-Arts, where he runs into Achille Laugé, a fellow southerner, in Cabanel's atelier. The two of them take the nude drawing classes of Adolphe Yvon. Later Maillol will say, "It was Laugé who put me on the right track."

1883

On January 16, following Gérome's advice, he finally enrolls in the sculpture section at the École des Arts Décoratifs. He works hard at modelling and reveals himself to be an excellent student.

Still Life with Pomegranate, 1890
Oil on canvas
21.5 x 27 cm

1884

Applies for and obtains a grant-in-aid from the Conseil Général of his native Department of the Pyrénées-Orientales. This stipendium, which varies between 200 and 400 francs, is awarded for several years running, until 1892, though it barely allows him to survive in Paris. He moves into an attic at 59 Rue de Seine. In fact, Maillol is almost totally destitute; he is chronically undernourished, has no relatives or benefactors he can turn to, and is in such poor health that he is hospitalized several times. Among other ailments, he suffers from articular rheumatism.

1885

Finally, on March 17, after several unsuccessful attempts, he passes the entrance examination at the Beaux-Arts and enrolls in the classes of Gérome, Laurens and, more importantly, Cabanel. During the next five years, he visits museums sedulously, particularly the Louvre where he has already done copies of paintings by Chardin, Fragonard, and Rembrandt. He is soon disappointed with the teaching at the Beaux-Arts, of which he had had high expectations. He finds himself left mostly to his own devices, with no instruction or master worthy of the name. He will later declare that he "learned nothing" at the Beaux-Arts. This is probably an exaggeration; Maillol did in fact receive a solid technical training at that academy. He worked hard during his years at the Beaux-Arts, but produced relatively little. It took him three years to complete his first painting there. He painted on canvases which he made by mounting jute sacks on stretchers.

Cover and title page of the catalogue for the group show at the Café Volpini, 1889. Maillol's friend Monfreid showed his work under the name Georges Daniel

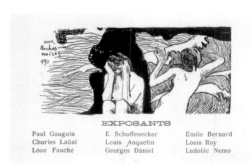

1888-1889

Exhibits a landscape at the Salon des Artistes Français. The following year he meets Bourdelle, at whose home he is often lodged and fed, as is Achille Laugé. The three men, all natives of the same area of the Midi, become fast friends. They pool their meagre resources and often work together. Maillol makes the acquaintance of Maurice Bouchor, who commissions him to do stage sets for his marionette theater on Rue Saint-Lazare. The pay is meagre – twenty francs for a five-meter canvas – but Maillol accepts the job anyway. Probably to justify his grant-in-aid, he makes a copy of Hyacinthe Rigaud's portrait of Philippe V at the Louvre and sends it to the prefect of the Pyrénées-Orientales. This same year, Daniel de Monfreid takes him to the Café Volpini to see an exhibition of paintings by the "Impressionist and Synthetist" Group. He discovers the avant-garde artists Van Gogh, Émile Bernard, Guillaumin, Schuffenecker and, chiefly, Gauguin. "Gauguin's painting was a revelation to me. Instead of enlightening me, the École des

The Crown of Flowers, 1889
Oil on canvas
130 x 161 cm
Josefowitz Collection

Beaux-Arts had thrown a veil over my eyes. Standing in front of the Pont-Aven paintings, I had a feeling that I too could work in that spirit. Right then I told myself that what I did would be good when it had Gauguin's approval."

1890

Exhibits a new picture at the Salon des Artistes Français: the portrait of Jeanne Faraill, whose great-uncle was the Perpignan-born sculptor Gabriel Faraill. The portrait is a commission, and it is thanks to Faraill, who lives in Paris, that Maillol obtains it. This year the Salon is split into two: the more traditional artists show their work at the Salon des Artistes Français; the more innovative ones, at the instigation of Puvis de Chavannes, Rodin, Meissonier, and Eugène Carrière, organize the Société Nationale des Beaux-Arts. Like many of his contemporaries, Maillol deeply admires Puvis de Chavannes, whose *Poor Fisherman* he copies. The influence of Gauguin is discernible as well in the canvases Maillol paints

The Washerwomen, 1889-1890
Oil on canvas
64 x 89 cm
Josefowitz Collection

between 1889 and 1890 – *The Washerwomen*, *Two Young Girls*, *The Crowned Child*, *Woman's Profile*, *Woman with Parasol*. The silhouettes of all of these figures stand out against a vaguely Impressionist background. Maillol meets the Hungarian painter, Rippl-Rónai, who will later introduce him to the Nabi group.

1892-1893

Becomes interested in tapestry-making, which he studies at the Cluny Museum, where he is fascinated by the *Lady with Unicorn* series. He exhibits his first "trial tapestry" the following year at the Salon of the Société Nationale des Beaux-Arts. That same year he sets up a petit-point tapestry workshop in Banyuls, employing two sisters, Angélique and Clotilde Narcisse, to work there. He uses only natural materials: the finest wool and pigments ground from plants which he himself gathers in the surrounding mountains.

Bust of Young Girl, 1890 – Oil on canvas – 55 x 46 cm

Glazed terracotta fountain, 1895

Clotilde Narcisse follows him to Paris, where they set up house together at number 282 Rue Saint-Jacques. The young couple is all but destitute, but find comfort at Bourdelle's. It is at the latter's studio that Maillol does his first sculpting. He carves a cradle for his friend's son, which Bourdelle's father assembles. Maillol and Clotilde are also regular guests of Daniel de Monfreid, who introduces the novice sculptor to a painter who is decorating a villa in Auteuil and who offers Maillol a job reproducing a palace interior in stucco. The wages are eleven francs per day. At the Salon de la Libre Esthétique in Brussels, Maillol exhibits a tapestry which Gauguin commends in an article for the review *Essais d'Art Libre*. Maillol's tapestry work, to which he devotes almost all of his time, is a severe strain on his eyesight and, after temporarily losing his sight, he resigns himself to giving up this art.

The Wave, 1895
Bronze
29 x 33 cm

1895

Exhibits a tapestry at the Salon of the Société Nationale des Beaux-Arts and begins his career as a sculptor. Executes his first sculptures in wood on themes derived from his tapestries (*Dancer, Woman Seated in a Meditative Attitude*), as well as a number of ceramic objects: several small mural fountains and *The Water Carriers*.

1896

Marries Clotilde on July 7; their only son is born on October 30. Exhibits a tapestry, three wood carvings, and a wax statuette at the Salon de la Société Nationale des Beaux-Arts, where the latter are pejoratively labelled *objets d'art*.

1897

Exhibits a tapestry and a vitrine of small sculptures at the Nationale, again under the label *objets d'art*. He is introduced to Princess Bibesco, who commissions a tapestry.

Maillol, Clotilde and their son Lucien photographed in Daniel de Monfreid's house

The Swing, 1896
Sketch for tapestry
Oil on cardboard
22 x 27 cm

Decorative Tapestry for a Chair,
ca. 1900
45 x 65 cm

Princess Bibesco, 1895
Bronze
15 x 14 x 9 cm

1899

Still in financial straits, Maillol and Clotilde move to Villeneuve-
Saint-Georges, near Paris. The rent is lower here, and for the first
time Maillol has a studio of his own. Exhibits the tapestry *The
Garden* at the Nationale. Meets Picasso. In regular touch with
some of the Nabi artists, whose group he will soon join.

1900

Receives friends at his Villeneuve-Saint-Georges house: Maurice
Denis, Ker-Xavier Roussel, Edouard Vuillard, Thadée Natanson,
Pierre Bonnard, Rippl-Rónai, and the poet Marc Lafargue. Shows
them terracotta and faience objects he has brought back from his
last visit to Banyuls. Vuillard introduces him to Ambroise Vollard, who buys several of his sculptures and has them cast in
bronze. In spite of this, the Maillols' financial situation remains
precarious. Maillol gives up woodcarving and begins working
with clay and bronze, producing some thirty statuettes in one year.
He begins work on the first *Crouching Woman*, which he will later

Self-Portrait (recto), ca. 1898 – Ink on paper – 29 x 21 cm

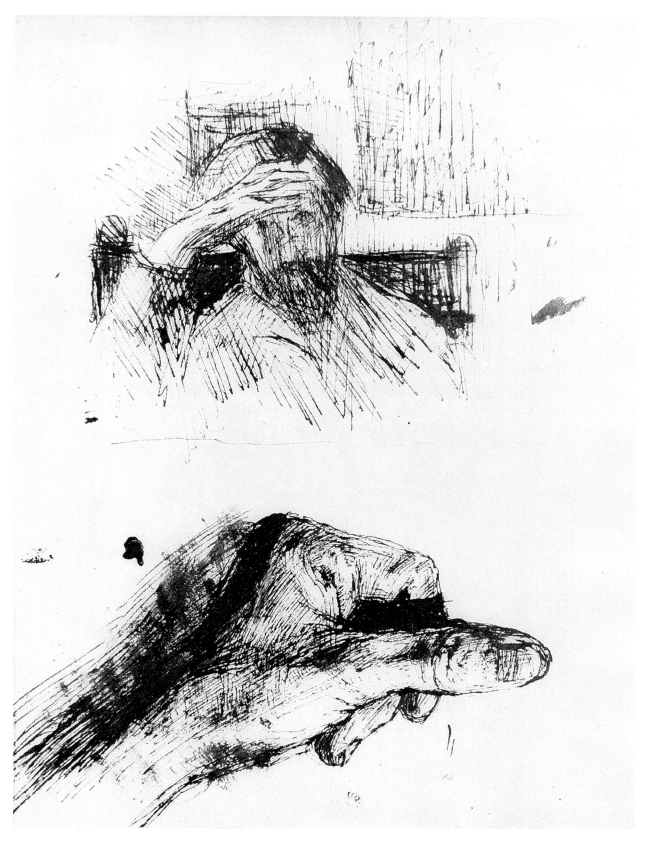

Self-Portrait (verso), ca. 1898 – Ink on paper – 29 x 21 cm

call *Serenity*, a large-scale study that will lead to the first version of *La Méditerranée*. Matisse helps him make the plaster mold for this study.

1902

Participates in a group show at Galerie Berthe Weil and has his first one-man show at Vollard's on Rue Laffitte from June 16-30, where he exhibits thirty-three works: tapestries, woodcarvings, an iron doorknocker, a gilt copper mantle clock, an enamel-ware wall fountain, a mirror, his son's cradle, and a number of sculptures in plaster, wood and bronze, including *Leda*. This last work is noticed

József Rippl-Rónai:
Portrait of Maillol, 1899
Paris, Musée d'Orsay

Two Seated Women, 1895
Bronze
H. 13 cm

165

Maurice Denis:
Adoration of the Magi, detail, 1904
Dijon, Musée des Beaux-Arts
From left to right: Maillol,
Sérusier, Vollard

Maillol in 1906 in front of the
plaster of La Méditerranée

by Octave Mirbeau, who eventually acquires it. Through his writings and efforts to obtain commissions for him, the writer and art critic will be a supporter of Maillol's throughout the sculptor's career. The one-man show is a great success. The critic Félicien Fagus devotes two separate articles to Maillol in *La Revue Blanche* (the January and August issues respectively).

1903
Maillol is mentioned in the catalogue of the Salon de la Société National des Beaux-Arts under both the sculpture and *objets d'art* headings. Exhibits the plaster bas-relief, *Woman Bathing*. Moves to Marly-le-Roi to be closer to his friends Maurice Denis, Roussel, and Vuillard. He first rents a house, then buys another (which he will later sell to one of Bourdelle's sons) and builds a studio, and soon after that yet another house, on a plot of land on the edge of a wood. Henceforth he will divide his time between Banyuls in the winter and Marly-le-Roi in summer. Zola dies, and Mirbeau proposes to ask Maillol to sculpt a memorial to the great writer. The other members of the Zola committee are opposed to this idea, especially Théodore Duret who demands "someone who's consumed with fire." "Those idiots want a patient," complains Mirbeau. In the end, the task of sculpting the monument is entrusted to Constantin Meunier and Alexandre Charpentier.

1904
First appearance at the Salon d'Automne. Meier-Graefe mentions Maillol in his study of modern art.

1905
The plaster of *La Méditerranée* is exhibited at the famous Salon d'Automne of the "Fauves" scandal, and attracts considerable notice. Maillol's career is launched. Three important articles are devoted to him: André Gide praises him for breathing new life into sculpture; Mirbeau publishes a long study on Maillol's renewal of the female image; and Maurice Denis links him to the great

Seated Torso with Drapery, 1896 – Bronze – 20.5 x 11.8 cm

Marthe Denis posing for Maillol,
ca. 1907

tradition of archaic Greek sculpture and Gothic art. Through Rodin, Maillol meets Count Kessler, who will become his main patron, at his dealer's, Ambroise Vollard. A member of one of the most distinguished German families, Kessler was said by some to be the bastard son of the Emperor Wilhelm II. A deeply cultivated man and a great humanist in the tradition of Humboldt, he championed Socialist ideas in the reactionary Germany of his day. His career as a diplomat gave him leisure to frequent artistic and literary circles. He received Einstein, Rilke, Gide, Paul Morand, Cocteau, Diaghilev, and Misia Sert. A man of vast wealth and great generosity, he was keenly interested in publishing and founded the famous Cranach Press. Kessler commissions Maillol to do *La Méditerranée* in stone, and to sculpt the high-relief *Desire*.

A committee is formed to select a sculptor for a memorial to Auguste Blanqui. Several of Maillol's friends – Octave Mirbeau, Maurice Denis, Francis Jourdain, and Henri Barbusse – persuade Clemenceau to approve Maillol's nomination. The result is the monumental statue *Action in Chains*. Maillol and Matisse become close friends and see each other daily.

Count Kessler's study at Weimar,
ca. 1909

1906

Exhibits a standing female figure at the Salon d'Automne. Becomes acquainted with Pierre Camo and Marc Lafargue, whom he meets at Vollard's.

1907

Completes the relief of *Desire* in lead and begins work on another statue for Count Kessler, *The Cyclist*. Sculpts a bust of Renoir at Cagnes. Watching Maillol at work, the great painter is inspired to take up sculpture himself.

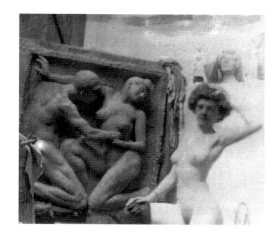

Desire, with model, ca. 1908
Photo by Harry Kessler

1908

Kessler invites Maillol, who has never travelled outside of France, to visit Greece with him and the poet Hugo von Hofmannsthal. Kessler and Maillol embark aboard the *Bremen* at Marseilles on April 25. They stop off at Naples and visit Pompeii and Mount Vesuvius. Five days later they reach Athens, where Hofmannsthal is waiting for them. Maillol admires the Propylaea, the Parthenon, and especially the examples of sixth-century BC sculpture he sees,

Maillol working on The Cyclist
with model Gaston Colin, 1907
Photos by Harry Kessler

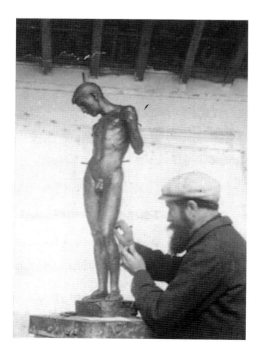

Maillol in 1907

such as the caryatids on the porch of the Erechteum. After returning to France, Maillol completes *The Cyclist.* He resumes work on *Night*, a major work he had begun in 1902. The Municipality of Puget-Théniers is shocked by the monument to Blanqui and cancels the unveiling, which had been scheduled to take place in October.

1909
Exhibits *Night* and *The Cyclist* at the Salon d'Automne.

1910
Kessler commissions him to illustrate Virgil's *Eclogues*, and Maillol undertakes to do this with a series of woodblocks. The translation is that of his friend Marc Lafargue. Maillol is dissatisfied with commercially available paper and decides to manufacture his own rag paper. This is the origin of "Montval" paper. "I detest illustrated books. I do them because I do not consider line engraving

Maillol at the Archaeological Museum in Olympus

Greek Landscape, 1908
Oil on canvas

Printer's mark of the "Cranach Presse" edition of Virgil's Eclogues

on wood to be illustration; drawings done in this way are the equivalent of typographical characters; to me, they are typography." To obtain a perfectly smooth surface, Maillol carves the woodblocks himself in pear wood. It takes him two years (1910-1912) to complete the illustrations for the book, which will only be published in 1925.

Pomona gets a highly favorable reception at the Salon d'Automne. The great Russian collector Ivan Morosov buys it and commissions *Summer*, *Spring*, and *Flora*, to make up the four *Seasons* which he installs in his town-house in Moscow, where Maurice Denis is at work on a series of frescos recounting *The Story of Psyche*. Maillol will complete the three statues in 1912. In 1910, he begins the preliminary work on a statue of a young girl walking in water. He will spend more than ten years on this figure, which will eventually become the sculpture *Île-de-France*. He is deeply depressed following the death of his aunt Lucie.

1911
Exhibits tapestries at Galerie Bernheim-Jeune.

Interior of Ivan Morosov's house in Moscow, with Flora and Spring

1912

Cézanne's closest friends form a committee to raise funds for a memorial to the painter, which they intend to present to his native Aix-en-Provence. The committee is headed by Frantz Jourdain, founder and president of the Salon d'Automne, and includes a number of Maillol's friends. Money is raised thanks to a public subscription and a sale of works by Bonnard, Vuillard, Matisse, Maurice Denis, and Maillol at Galerie Bernheim-Jeune. Maillol is commissioned to sculpt the monument – which is then rejected by the Municipality of Aix-en-Provence.

1913

Kessler rents a barn for Maillol at Montval, one kilometer from Marly-le-Roi, where the sculptor installs a paper manufacturing shop. After Maillol's first trial samples (which he produces in 1906 under Matisse's eyes) are improved, Kessler wants to make the resulting high-quality paper available commercially. Maillol puts his nephew Gaspard in charge of the Montval manufacture, which is eventually sold to the paper firm of Montgolfier. The paper's

Small Flora, 1911
Bronze
H. 66 cm

Interior of Ivan Morosov's house
in Moscow, with Summer and Pomona

Monument to the War Dead of Céret

Monument to the War Dead of Elne

watermark consists of Maillol and Kessler's initials surmounted by *La Méditerranée.*

1914

Shortly before the outbreak of World War I, Kessler cables Maillol advising him to bury his statues. This friendly advice lands Maillol in serious trouble. The public prosecutor in nearby Versailles issues a search warrant, as a first step to having Maillol arrested for treason. In the end, the investigating judge dismisses the charge.

1915

Two hostile articles about Maillol appear in the right-wing *L'Action Française* and in *Le Figaro.* Kessler and his magazine *Simplicissimus* are violently attacked as well, and his patronage of Maillol is denounced. The sculptor's son Lucien is mobilized. For the first time since he has come to Paris, Maillol, who wants to stay close to him, does not winter in Banyuls.

1918

Begins work on *Venus with Necklace*, which he will complete ten years later.

1919

The Municipality of Céret commissions him to sculpt a monument to the war dead. He begins work on the stone the following year.

1921

Exhibits the *Draped Bather* at the Salon d'Automne. The first version of the statue is a nude, the second, a torso.

1922

Unveiling of the Céret monument to the war dead. The town of Port-Vendres commissions him to do a war monument for its municipality, which is unveiled the following year. Maillol exhibits a stone *Bust of a Young Girl* and a bronze *Pomona* at the Salon d'Automne.

1923

Receives his first commission from the French state: a marble version of *La Méditerranée*.

1925

Thanks to the intervention of the French president, the *Monument to Cézanne*, which had been rejected by the City of Aix, is acquired by the City of Paris, even before it is decided where to install it. Maillol completes *Île-de-France*. The town of Elne, in the Department of the Pyrénées-Orientales, commissions him to do a monument to the war dead. Several important books on Maillol appear. First one-man show in the United States, at the Albright Gallery in Buffalo.

1927

Death of his friend Marc Lafargue.

1928

Exhibits the plaster of the *Venus with Necklace* at the Salon d'Automne, where Rodin's famous bronze of Balzac is also displayed. Maillol exhibits in London and Berlin. Travels to Germany and meets Einstein.

1929

In October, following a press campaign, the stone version of the *Monument to Cézanne* is finally installed in the Tuileries gardens, between the double ramps leading to the terrace of the Orangerie.

Armless Île-de-France
Bronze
H. 167 cm

Edouard Vuillard: Portrait of Maillol, 1930-1935
Distemper – 115 x 119 cm – Musée d'Art Moderne de la Ville de Paris
Photothèque des Musées de la Ville de Paris

Maillol finishing the Monument to the War Dead of Banyuls

1930

Works on the Banyuls monument for the war dead. Accepts a commission to sculpt a monument to Claude Debussy. Begins work on the central figure in the group of the *Three Nymphs*. Participates in the "Art Vivant" exhibition. Visits Germany with Count Kessler. Goes to the latter's home at Weimar, then to Berlin (where he discovers the Pergamon Museum), Frankfurt, Erfurt, Iena, and Naumburg. Museum directors, gallery owners and collectors greet him with admiration wherever he goes. Meets Max Lieberman and Einstein.

Funeral Monument in Basel cemetery

1931

Publication of Émile Verhaeren's book *Belle Chair*, illustrated with lithographs by Maillol. A large celebration organized in April at Banyuls on the occasion of the sculptor's seventieth birthday.

1933

January, opening of a Maillol exhibition at the Brummer Gallery in New York. The *Monument to Debussy* is unveiled in the gardens of the municipal library of Saint-Germain-en-Laye. Unveiling of the *Monument to the War Dead* at Banyuls. A Maillol retrospective is organized at the Kunsthalle in Basel, Switzerland, and receives universally favorable reviews. Hitler seizes power in Germany. As a declared opponent of the Nazi regime, Count Kessler is obliged to leave Germany and seek refuge in France.

Maillol's studio in 1934. Photo Brassaï

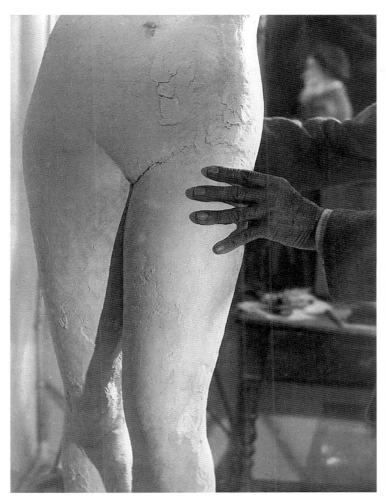

Maillol Working on Harmony, 1943. Photo Karquel

1934

With the help of his son, Maillol installs the funeral monument in lead commissioned by Mrs. Hoffmann in a cemetery in Basel. The sculptor receives Jean Cassou who calls on him on behalf of Georges Huisman, director of the Beaux-Arts, who wishes to acquire several of his bronzes for the French State.

Matisse in Maillol's studio

1935

The City of Paris acquires *Île-de-France* in bronze. Publication of Ovid's *Art of Love*, with woodcuts and lithographs by Maillol.

In Maillol's studio, 1936
Photo Brassaï

Maillol in Florence

1936

Travels to Italy with his friend the sculptor Pimienta. Visits Milan, Florence, and Rome, where he is particularly struck by the Sistine Chapel. Decides to take up painting again. Studies the art of one of his favorite painters, Raphael, and the statues and frescos of Michelangelo.

1937

Completes the *Three Nymphs in the Meadow*. Concurrently with the World's Fair, a large exhibition entitled "Les Maîtres de l'Art Indépendant" is held at the Petit Palais in Paris. No less than three rooms are devoted entirely to Maillol's work. Maillol works on the stone version of *The Mountain* for the Museum of Modern Art in Paris. The "Cranach Presse" edition of *Daphnis and Chloe* appears with Maillol's woodcuts. Judith Cladel's biography is published.

Death of Count Kessler in Marseilles.

Maillol goes back to painting. Photo Karquel

Maillol drawing and painting
Photos Karquel

Paintings in the Marly-le-Roi
studio
Photo Brassaï

Maquette for Air, 1938
Photo John Rewald

1938

Sculpts *Air* in stone for the City of Toulouse, as a memorial for the pilots of the Aéropostale killed in the line of duty. Receives a commission to sculpt a memorial to the writer Henri Barbusse.

1939

Illustrates Verlaine's *Chansons pour Elle*. Begins work on the drawings for Virgil's *Georgics*, which will only be published in 1950. Publication of John Rewald's book on Maillol at Éditions Hypérion in Paris. The Institute of Modern Art in Boston organizes a joint Despiau-Maillol show. Maillol painting again, becomes interested in fresco-making. In August, Ambroise Vollard dies in a car crash. Outbreak of World War II. Maillol leaves Marly-le-Roi for Banyuls in September.

1940-1941

Publication of Ronsard's *Livre des Folastreries*, illustrated by Maillol. The Henri Barbusse memorial committee is unable to raise sufficient funds to pay for a monument to the writer. Maillol

Woodcut for Virgil's Georgics

Maillol and The Mountain, 1936
Photo Brassaï

continues to work on the project at his own expense, transforming it into *The River*. Jean Cassou and Georges Huisman call on him. Maillol in Banyuls when France surrenders to Germany. Vuillard dies during the exodus. Fleeing the Germans, Maillol's friend Wanda Landowska comes to stay in Banyuls. Maillol works on his last sculpture, *Harmony*. His model Dina Vierny joins him in Banyuls, making it possible for him to pursue his work on

Dina Vierny and one of Maillol's sculptures. Photo Brassaï

Harmony, which will occupy him for the next four years. Many versions of *Harmony* are destroyed. Maillol keeps plasters of four finished versions, as well as a headless standing torso, a torso with head, a head which served as a study for the treatment of the hair of the definitive version, and a mask. Maillol devotes several hours a day to painting, sculpting, and drawing. Catalogues his œuvre with the help of Dina Verny. Dina Vierny informs him of her activities in the French Resistance and her efforts to smuggle persons wanted by the Germans across the border into Spain. Maillol offers to let her use his studio at Puig del Mas as a way station, and shows her a safe path over the mountains. The first clandestine network across the Spanish border will be called the "Maillol network." These events are described in Daniel Benedite's book, *La filière marseillaise*, and are documented at the Museum of

Portrait of Maillol

Dina Vierny and Maillol
Photo Louis Carré

The Marly-le-Roi studio, ca. 1932. Photo Brassaï

the Holocaust in Washington, D.C., notably with a photograph (dated 1940) of Dina Vierny in the Pyrenees and a letter from Varian Fry, the American consul in Marseilles who organized the American Rescue Center and helped a large number of people to escape from the Germans.

Maillol painting
Photo Karquel

27 February, 1967

Dear Albert,

I have signed a contract to write a new paperback book on our "OPERATION EMERGENCY RESCUE" (the working title) of nearly 27 years ago, and the publisher wants me to add something for which I'll need to call on your memory, apparently. That is the story of the Aristide Maillol-Dina Vierny route over the Pyrenees, from Maillol's studio in Banyuls to the frontier station at Port Bou. Who made the contact, and approximately when? Who were some of the best-known refugees who escaped over that route? Any interesting details?

You remember, I'm sure, that we used to send certain refugees to Maillol's studio, that Maillol himself had shown Dina Vierny, his buxom young model, the footpath over the Pyrenees to Port Bou, and that, on moonless nights, Dina used to lead the refugees over the Pyrenees by that route, to avoid the French border patrols.

But how did all this come about? There is no use my writing to Dina. She is busy running a successful art gallery in the rue Jacob, and never answers letters. I wrote to Daniel Benedite, and he answered: "The Maillol/Dina route was the very first to be used by the American Rescue Center, and I think that the network was set up before the time when J. Gemahling and myself were associated with your activities.

It seems to me that the person who is in the best position to tell you about this, besides Dina of course, would be Hirschmann-Beamish.

Can you?

My affectionate greetings to you both!

(Document published with the kind permission of the Varian Fry Papers, Rare Book and Manuscript Library, Columbia University, New York.)

1942

Maillol's house and studio at Marly-le-Roi unoccupied since the sculptor withdrew to Banyuls in September 1939. The sculptor is

Portrait of Maillol

deeply attached to Marly, where he has been living since the turn of the century and where he has received many friends, artists, and admirers of his work. Far from Marly, he feels isolated. Moreover, he worries about that fate of the many works, especially the small sculptures, he has left behind in his Marly studio. But returning to Marly means crossing into the occupied zone, and to Maillol, by now in his eighty-first year, this seems too complicated to do on his own.

His desire to see his home in Marly again leads him to accept an invitation to the opening of Arno Brekker's show at the Orangerie in Paris in 1942. A German officer, Lt. Heller, comes to fetch him and take him to Paris. In his book *Un Allemand à Paris* (Paris: Le Seuil, 1981), he recalls that Brekker was very eager to have Maillol attend his show. "Somebody had to go and get him at Collioures and accompany him on the journey. I was glad to be picked for this mission. The permit he needed to cross the line of demarcation had not yet been issued." On the way, Heller asks Maillol what he thinks of Brekker's work. The sculptor replies evasively, "Oh, I've heard that it is grandiose." Indeed, Brekker is a sculptor who goes in for monumental, not to say grandiloquent, effects — not at all the sort of sculpture that appeals to Maillol's tastes. At the opening, on May 22, 1942, Maillol rejoices at encountering a number of artists he has been completely out of touch with since the beginning of the war: Van Dongen, Despiau, de Segonzac, Vlaminck, and Derain. Heller comments that Maillol "had agreed to come, without giving much thought to the fact that his presence at the opening might seriously compromise him." And the fact is that Maillol has not envisaged the dire personal consequences this visit to Paris is to have. Much later, a number of people unacquainted with Maillol the man and the artist, will come to the conclusion, after reading accounts of the Brekker opening, that Maillol collaborated with the Germans — which was of course never the case. Maillol's contacts with Germany go as far back as 1905. All his German friends and collectors, like Count Kessler, were forced into exile by the Nazis. Maillol was a pacifist and a humanist, like

Renoir, and it is simply grotesque to suggest that he had any affinity for Hitler's totalitarian and militaristic regime.

1943

Maillol still working on *Harmony*, which he will never complete.

1944

September 15, grievously wounded in a car accident on the way to see the painter Raoul Dufy. September 27, Maillol dies in his home.

The Monument to Cézanne in the Tuileries Gardens, 1964
Photo Maywald

1963

Dina Vierny proposes removing the *Monument to Cézanne* from the Tuileries Gardens and relocating it in the Museum of Modern Art. André Malraux, the Minister of Culture, agrees. She donates an important collection of Maillol sculptures to the French State. Malraux decides to have them installed in the Tuileries Gardens.

1964

Eighteen sculptures in bronze and lead are installed in the Tuileries, near the Carrousel.

1977

Dina Vierny decides to open up her collection to the public and establishes the Maillol Museum at the Hôtel Bouchardon, 59 and 61 Rue de Grenelle, in Paris.

1983

The Maillol Museum - Dina Vierny Foundation is approved by the French State.

1994

The Maillol Museum opens its doors to the public.

The Maillol Museum
59-61 Rue de Grenelle, Paris
Fountain of the Four Seasons
by Bouchardon
Photo A. Brunelle

MAJOR ONE-MAN SHOWS

1902 Paris, Galerie Ambroise Vollard.

1911 Paris, Bernheim-Jeune & Co. Les Tapisseries d'Aristide Maillol. January 23 - February 1.

1924 Berlin, Flechtheim Gallery. Preface to catalogue by Harry Kessler.

1925 Buffalo, New York, The Buffalo Fine Arts Academy, Albright Art Gallery. Sculpture and Drawings by Aristide Maillol, 1925-1926. Prefaces to catalogue by Augustus John and Anna Glenny Dunbar. November 15 - December 15.

1926 New York, Brummer Gallery. Sculpture and Drawings by Aristide Maillol. January 18 - February 13.

1927 Rochester, New York, Memorial Art Gallery. Sculpture and Drawings by Aristide Maillol. Catalogue. April.

1928 London, Goupil Gallery, October.
Berlin, Flechtheim Gallery. Catalogue. November-December.

1929 Brussels, Galerie Giroux. Maillol. Preface to catalogue by Harry Kessler. February.

1933 Basel, Kunsthalle. Aristide Maillol. Prefaces to catalogue by Ernst Suter and Otto Roos.
New York, Brummer Gallery. Sculpture by Maillol. Preface to catalogue by Conger Goodyear. January-February.

1937 Paris, Petit Palais.

1938 New York, Valentine Gallery. *Venus*, a bronze by Aristide Maillol. Exhibited with works by Georges Rouault and other Twentieth Century French masters.

1939 New York, Buchholz Gallery. Aristide Maillol. Preface to catalogue by John Rewald. January 31 - February 21.

1940 Chicago, The Arts Club. Aristide Maillol. December.

1941 Paris, Galerie Louise Carré. Maillol: dessins et pastels. Preface to catalogue by Maurice Denis. December.

1942 New York, Weihe Gallery. Aristide Maillol: drawings, prints, sculpture. January 5-31.

1944 Basel, Kunsthalle. Gedächtnis-Schau Aristide Maillol. November 25 - December 31.

1945 Buffalo, New York, The Buffalo Fine Arts Academy, Albright Art Gallery. Aristide Maillol. Catalogue, with preface by Andrew C. Richie, and excerpts of interviews with the sculptor from Judith Cladel's biography, *Aristide Maillol, sa vie, son œuvre, ses idées.* April 14 - May 23. New York, Buchholz Gallery. Aristide Maillol, 1861-1944. June 6-30.

1947 Paris, Galerie Dina Vierny. Hommage à Maillol.
Paris, Galerie Charpentier. Rétrospective Maillol. Catalogue, with prefaces by Jules Romains and Waldemar George.
Paris, Petit Palais. Aristide Maillol. Catalogue. May.
Copenhagen, Ny Carlsberg Glyptotek. Aristide Maillol. Preface to catalogue by Haavard Rostrup.
Stockholm, Blanch's Konstagalleri. Aristide Maillol, 1861-1944: Gobelänger, skulpturer, oljemalningar, pasteller och teckningar. Preface to catalogue by Gustaf Engwall. September-October.
Zurich, Kunsthaus. Maillol: Gemälde und Werkzeichnungen. September-November.

1950 Munich, Karin Hielscher Gallery. Aristide Maillol. Preface to catalogue by John Rewald. November 1950 - January 1951.

1951 New York, Buchholz Gallery, Curt Valentin. Aristide Maillol: 1861-1944. Catalogue, with excerpt from Judith Cladel's biography. February-March.

1954 Stockholm, Blanch's Konstagalleri. Aristide Maillol skulpturer, teckningar, grafik. Catalogue. March-April.

1955 London, Gimpel Gallery. Aristide Maillol.

1956 Marseilles, Musée Cantini. Aristide Maillol. Preface to catalogue by Jean Cassou. July-August.

1958 New York, Rosenberg Gallery, and 10 leading American museums (1958-1960). Catalogue.

1961 Paris, Musée National d'Art Moderne. Rétrospective pour le centenaire de la naissance de Maillol. Catalogue.
Amsterdam, Stedelijk Museum. Aristide Maillol. Catalogue.

1962 Frankfurt, Kunstverein. Aristide Maillol.
Munich, Haus der Kunst.
Stuttgart, Kunstverein.

1963 Stockholm, Pierre Gallery. Catalogue.
Helsinki, Artek Gallery. Catalogue.
Tokyo, Kokuritso Seijo Bijutsukan (Museum of Western Art). Maillol retrospective. Catalogue.

1964 Neuchâtel, Switzerland, Musée des Beaux-Arts. Aristide Maillol. Catalogue. June-September.

1967 Stockholm, Pierre Gallery. Aristide Maillol. Catalogue. November-December.

1970 New York, Perls Galleries. Preface to catalogue by John Rewald. March 18 - April 18.
Nice, Palais de la Méditerranée. Maillol. Catalogue. December 1970 - February 1971.

1971 Brest, Palais des Arts et de la Culture. Catalogue. Summer.
London, Gimpel Gallery. Maillol. Catalogue. October 26 - November 20.

1973 Caracas, Conkright Gallery. Maillol. Catalogue. May.

1974 Rochechouart, France, Centre artistique et littéraire de Rochechouart. Catalogue, with prefaces by John Rewald and Michel Hoog. March 29 - June 3.
Japan. Itinerant exhibition. Aristide Maillol. Hyogo-Kobe, Japan, Prefectorial Museum of Modern Art. Catalogue. October 10 - December 10.
Hiroshima, Prefectorial Museum of Art. November 10 - December 22.

1975 Ehime-Matsuyama, Japan, Prefectorial Museum. January 5-19.
Kitakyushu, Japan, City Museum. January 25 - February 23.

Kanazawa, Japan, MRO Hall. March 10 - April 3.
Japan, Mitsukoshi Gallery. April 15-20.
London, Gimpel Gallery. Maillol. Catalogue. March 11 - April 12.
New York, The Solomon R. Guggenheim Foundation. Catalogue. 1975-1976.

1976 Tokyo, Contemporary Sculpture Center. Catalogue. June 7-19.
Osaka, Japan, Contemporary Sculpture Center. Catalogue. June 7-19.
Caracas, Adler-Castillo Gallery. Catalogue. November 7-21.

1978 Baden-Baden, Germany, Staatliche Kunsthalle. Maillol. Catalogue, with preface by Hans Albert Peters and a text by John Rewald. June 17 - September 3.

1979 Perpignan, France, Palais des Rois de Majorque. Maillol. Catalogue, preface by Bernard Nicolau, text by John Rewald. March 15 - May 30.
Barcelona, "La Caixa" Cultural Center. September 27 - November 15.

1980 Stuttgart, Valentin Gallery. September.

1984 Yamanashi, Japan, Departmental Museum of Fine Arts. April 7 - May 9. Hiroshima, Museum of Fine Arts. May 12 - June 17. Kumamoto, Japan, Prefectorial Museum of Fine-Arts. June 23 - July 29. Kanazawa, Japan, Ishikawa Prefectorial Museum of Fine Arts. August 4-27. Matsuama, Japan, Ehime Prefectorial Museum of Fine-Arts. September 8-30. Kobe, Japan, Hyogo Prefectorial Museum of Fine Arts. October 5 - November 4. Tokyo, Isetan Museum. November 9-27.

1987 Paris, Galerie Dina Vierny. Maillol, les 40 ans de la Galerie. Catalogue, preface by Pierre Cabanne, text by Bertrand Lorquin.

1994 Mexico, San Carlos Museum.
Saint-Tropez, France, Musée de l'Annonciade. Japan, itinerant exhibition. Tokyo, September 1 to mid-october. Mitsukoshi Museum, early November-early December. Hokkaido, The Hokkaido Hakodate Museum of Art.

1995 Takamatsu City Museum of Art.
Chiba Prefectural Museum of Art.
Fukushima Prefectural Museum of Art.
Himeji City Museum of Art.

MAJOR WORKS ON MAILLOL

Mirbeau Octave: *Aristide Maillol*, Paris, Crès, 1921.
Denis Maurice: *A. Maillol*, Paris, Crès, 1925.
Kuhn Alfred: *Aristide Maillol*, Leipzig, Seemann, 1925.
Zervos Christian: *Aristide Maillol*, Paris, L'Art d'Aujourd'hui, 1925.
Lafargue Marc: *Aristide Maillol, sculpteur et lithographe*, Paris, Frapier, 1925.
Camo Pierre: *Aristide Maillol*, Paris, Librairie Gallimard, 1926.
George Waldemar: *Le miracle de Maillol*, Paris, Album Druet, 1927.
Lafargue Marc: *Grande ode au jardin de Marly et à Aristide Maillol*, Paris, Cité Falguières, 1928.
Sentenac Paul: *Aristide Maillol*, Peyre, 1936.
René-Jean: *Maillol*, Album «Galerie d'Estampes», Paris, Braun, 1936.
Cladel Judith: *Maillol, sa vie, son œuvre, ses idées*, Paris, Grasset, 1937.
Dormoy Marie: *Maillol*, Paris, Arts et Métiers graphiques, 1937.
Rewald John: *Les ateliers de Maillol*, Colmar, Le point, november 1938.
Rewald John: *Maillol*, Paris - London - New York, Hypérion, 1939.
Appel Heinrich: *Das Meisterwerk Maillol*, Basel, 1940.
Denis Maurice et Du Colombier Pierre: *Maillol - Dessins et pastels*, Paris, Louis Carré, 1942.
Payro Julio: *Aristide Maillol*, Editorial, Buenos Aires, Poseidon, 1942.
Rewald John: *The woodcuts of Aristide Maillol*, A complete catalogue, New York, Pantheon Books, 1943.
Valéry Paul, Perret Auguste, Denis Maurice, Du Colombier Pierre: *Maillol*, Paris, Les publications techniques, October 8, 1943.
Lafargue M., Mirbeau O., Camo P., Girou J.: *Aspect de Maillol*, Albi, 1945.
Ritchie Andrew C.: *Aristide Maillol 1861-1944*, Buffalo, Albright Art Gallery, 1945.
Bouvier Marguerite: *Aristide Maillol*, Lausanne, Éditions Marguerat, 1945.
Camo Pierre, Susplugas André, Frère Henri, Pons Joseph-Sébastien, Masse Ludovic: *Maillol*, Cahier des amis de l'Art, n° 10, 1946.
Roy Claude: *Maillol vivant*, Geneva, Pierre Cailler, 1947.
Carbonneaux Jean: *Maillol*, Paris, Éditions Braun, 1949.

Romains Jules: *Maillol*, Paris, 1940.
Camo Pierre: *Maillol, mon ami*, Lausanne, Éditions du Grand-Chêne, Henri Kaeser, 1950.
Rewald John: *Aristide Maillol*, Paris, Éditions Braun, 1950.
Ternovetz Boris: *Aristide Maillol*, Milano, Ulrico Hoepli Editore, 1950.
Remsshardt G.: *Aristide Maillol, Gefilde der Liebe*, Feldafing, 1954.
Kaestner E.: *Aristide Maillol, Hirtenleben*, Wiesbaden, Insel Verlag.
Frère Henri: *Conversations de Maillol*, Geneva, Éditions Pierre Cailler, 1956.
Uhde-Bernays Hermann: *Aristide Maillol*, Dresden, 1957.
Linnkamp Rolf: *Aristide Maillol und der goldene Schnitt der Fläche*, Hamburg, 1957.
Linnekamp Rolf: *Aristide Maillol*, Hamburg, 1957.
Masin Jiri: *Aristide Maillol*, Prague, 1960.
Hackelsberger Berthold: *La Méditerranée*, Stuttgart, 1960.
Linnekamp Rolf: *Aristide Maillol*, Munich, Bruckmann, 1960.
Hoetink H. R.: *Aristide Maillol, la Méditerranée*, 1963.
George Waldemar: *Aristide Maillol et l'âme de la sculpture*, Neuchâtel, Éditions Ides et Calendes, 1964.
Puig René: "La vie misérable et glorieuse d'Aristide Maillol", *Tramontane 49*, 1965.
Guérin Marcel: *Catalogue raisonné de l'œuvre gravé et lithographié d'Aristide Maillol*, 2 volumes, Geneva, Pierre Cailler, 1965.
Chevalier Denys: *Maillol*, Paris, Flammarion, 1970.
George Waldemar: *Maillol*, Éditions d'art, Arted, 1971.
Petrotchouk O.: *Maillol*, Moscow Art Editions, 1977.
Hans Albert Peters: *Maillol staatliche Kunsthalle*, (catalogue) Baden-Baden, 1978.
Kazuo Anazawa: *Maillol*, (catalogue of Maillol exhibition in Japan), 1984.
Vierny Dina, Lorquin Bertrand: *Autour de la Méditerranée*, Paris, Musée d'Orsay, 1986.
Bouille Michel, *Maillol, la femme toujours recommencée*, Paris, Éditions Éole, 1989.
Lorquin Bertrand: *Maillol aux Tuileries*, Paris, Éditions Adam Biro, 1991.

LIST OF ILLUSTRATIONS

All of the works reproduced here, except where a different provenance is mentioned, belong to the Dina Vierny Collection and the Maillol Museum - Dina Vierny Foundation. Most of the photographs, except those bearing a special mention, are by Jean Alex Brunelle.

Separations and printing by

IRL IMPRIMERIES RÉUNIES LAUSANNE S.A.